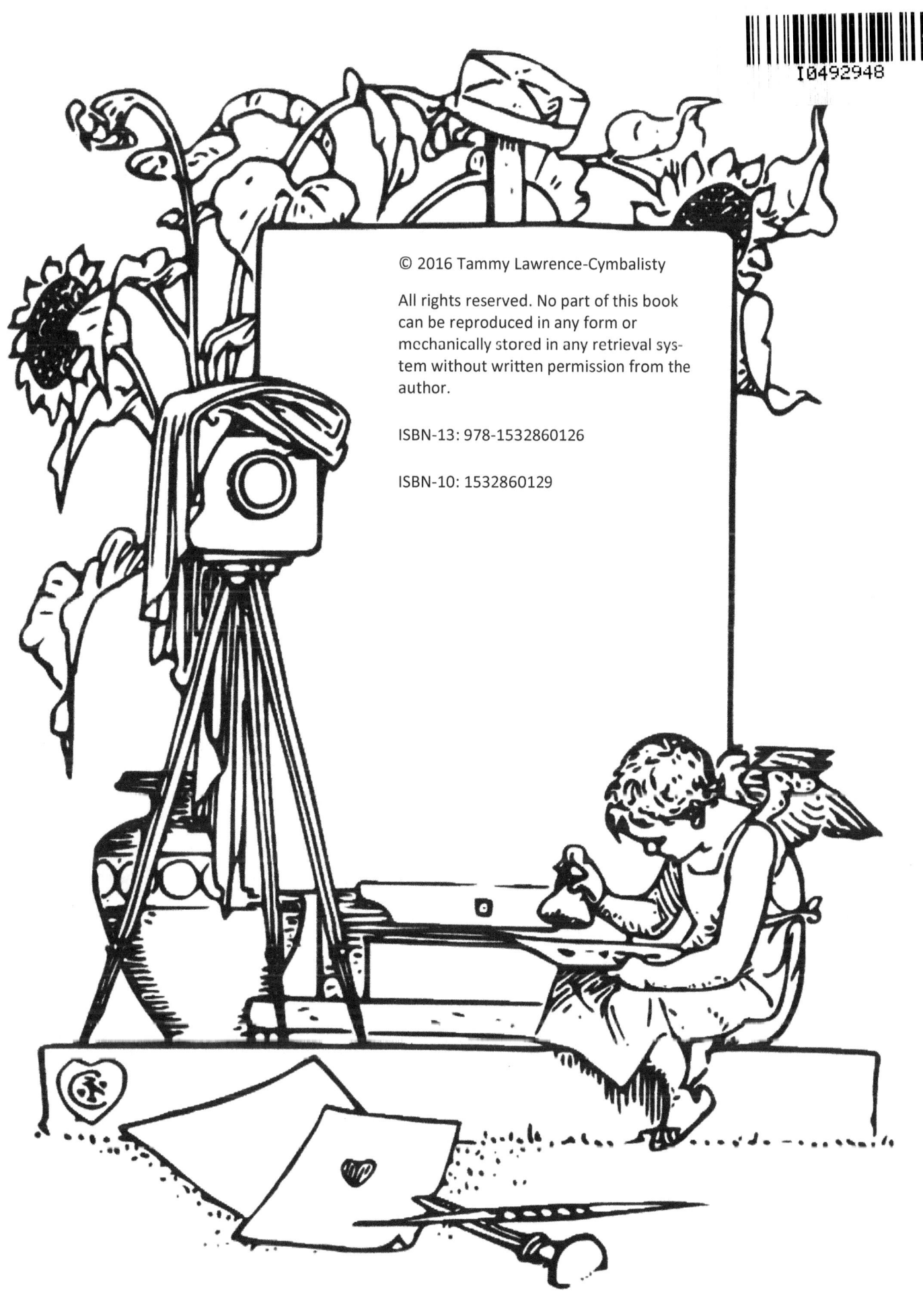

ISBN-13: 978-1532860126

ISBN-10: 1532860129

I0492948

This Stage of Grief:

Memory, Colouring and Workbook.

.

I'm sorry for your loss.

When we loose a loved one our whole world changes. Possibly the Police arrived at your door to tell you or a family member sat you down, you may have received the dreaded 3am phone call, a text or maybe you read the news on a social media site; from the instant we hear about the loss of someone we love we are sent into a state of shock and trauma. If you were close to them saying you are shocked feels like understatement. This life changing loss and the grieving that follows is what brings this book to you today.

According to therapists the stages of grief are: denial, anger, bargaining, depression and acceptance. They do not come in any logical order. They will bounce around in your mind until you come to terms (acceptance) with your loss and begin the journey forward with them tucked close to your heart.

I liken the stages to waves in the ocean that come and go. Some days the waves are small, other times much larger and then the tsunami-wave-days; the ones you wonder if you'll ever be able to get back up from or move forward from.

People have the greatest of intentions, but sometimes they'll say things that set you off. I recall one day I was going through a very hard day. The weather was gorgeous but my feelings didn't match. Someone said, with much enthusiasm, "How could anyone be having a bad day on a day like this!?" I knew the answer for me, but didn't wish to share. They had no idea what I was going through.

Maybe you've heard things like: "It happened for a reason." Or "They are in a better place now." The things some will say to you will bring up intense moments of emotion; some good, but mostly not. Grieving is not easy nor is it fast. Healing takes time. A lot of time in most cases. And it is as individual as we are.

You are in a time of great transition. You're loved one has passed. And I encourage you to be with this stage of grief; wherever you may be in this moment.

Whatever stage you are in welcome it. I know that sounds challenging, but the only way through it is to be with what is. Cease trying to control the outcome of any emotions that come up and just let yourself be with whatever experience is now. Good or bad from a discernment perspective; give yourself the space to grieve.

Expand into this moment. Allow. Breathe. Heal.

Most days this will not be an easy process. Allow this book to help you along this most difficult journey.

During a time of deep grieving myself I had someone say, "You are so blessed to have shared the entire life of this individual; the beauty of their life, the suffering, their challenges, their successes... all of it." At that point I didn't view it as beautiful. Maybe I would one day but from the pain of that moment I couldn't see it. It was the furthest thing from beautiful. It was all too much.

You may find yourself revisiting the days, the hours, the months, all of the words spoken or the events that lead up to your loss. The largest question for many, especially if the death was unexpected, is why? Why did it have to happen like this? Why did it have to be this way? Why? We may never know the answers.

In time you'll realize revisiting all of the moments, especially pain-filled ones, is not serving you. You can not change the fact they are gone. You must move forward as life does go on. But you can be here now and be open to receive how you are feeling in this moment; not supressing but allowing and being OK with where you are at today even if that doesn't fit a mould of where someone else wants you to be.

Forgive a lot. Forgive those who mention the loss in passing; those who bring it up in a way you not prepared for or in a way you are not ready to deal with. Their reality is not yours. They may not have a clue where you are at. Forgive them. Again and again and just allow yourself to be. Realize what they are saying is their experience and where you are could be totally different. They don't understand. How can they? They don't have your life experience. You will deal with things in your own time in your own way and no one can change that for you. Some days, some hours it will all be Ok. Other times it will not.

There will be angels in disguise. People who will save you in the moment. The inevitable meltdowns that come randomly and in the most unexpected of public places. Those who will pull you back into this moment and away from your grief. But it will still be there waiting in your private moments for you to journey through.

I implore you as you work through this stage of grief, whichever one you are in, to be with it; allow yourself to feel whatever comes up however pain-filled.

Cry. Scream. Be silent.

Give yourself permission to 'be' with you; experience the now. Feelings will change. Your experience will change, but today you have every right to experience where you are at. No one can change that.

Feel. Love. Honour.

It is the deepest of love that brings you to this moment. Regardless of what is being said to you allow yourself to feel this way; to experience this great loss, your way.

Know you are loved and have loved. The pain of today will become a part of you so grand it will forever change your experience. It already has. No one on this earth knows what your relationship was like with your loved one; except for you. And yes you were blessed to have know them and shared a part of this walk with them.

As you walk through this stage of grief remember the saying, "This too shall pass." Give yourself whatever time, energy and space you need. It is a process.

Many pages of this book are open for you to journal in, areas to add your thoughts or feelings of today. There are colouring pages, pages to honour your loved ones memory and pages to work through this stage of grief. Maybe you could glue a picture of them onto the page? Or maybe add affirmations or messages you wish them to receive. Whatever you do feel guided to do in order to honour your loved one and work through how you are feeling in the moment. So be it.

I would suggest placing a piece of paper (you could also choose waxed paper) behind the pictures particularly if you are choosing wet mediums to prevent any bleed-through. The pictures have a page between them to help with this additionally (potential journaling place?). However if you, like me, enjoy using acrylics or water-colour you may need the additional support for the page.

Wishing you sympathy in this time of challenge.

Be in this moment and know you are not alone.

Much love,

Tammy

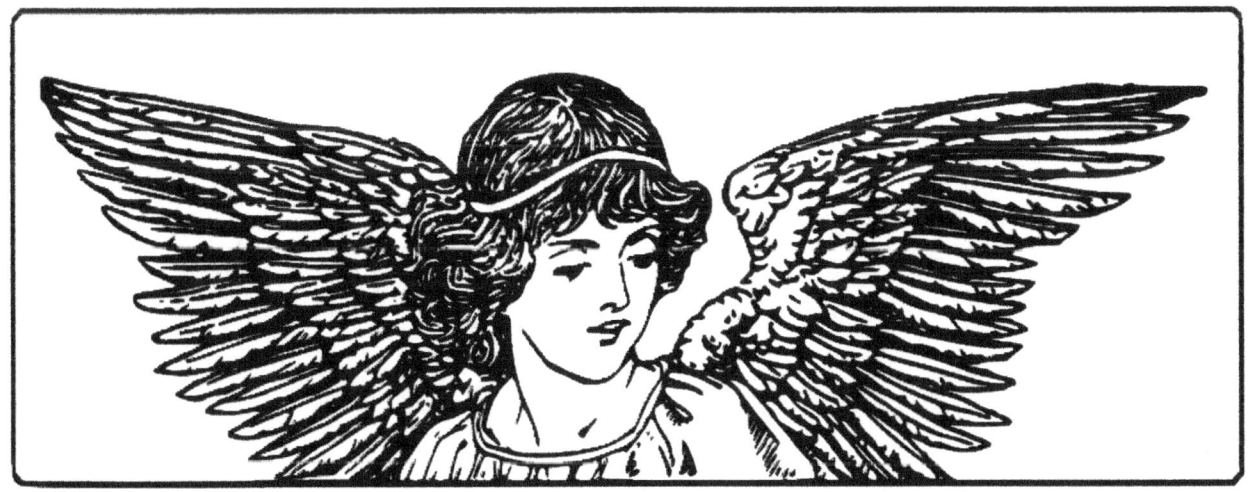

Favourite Memories

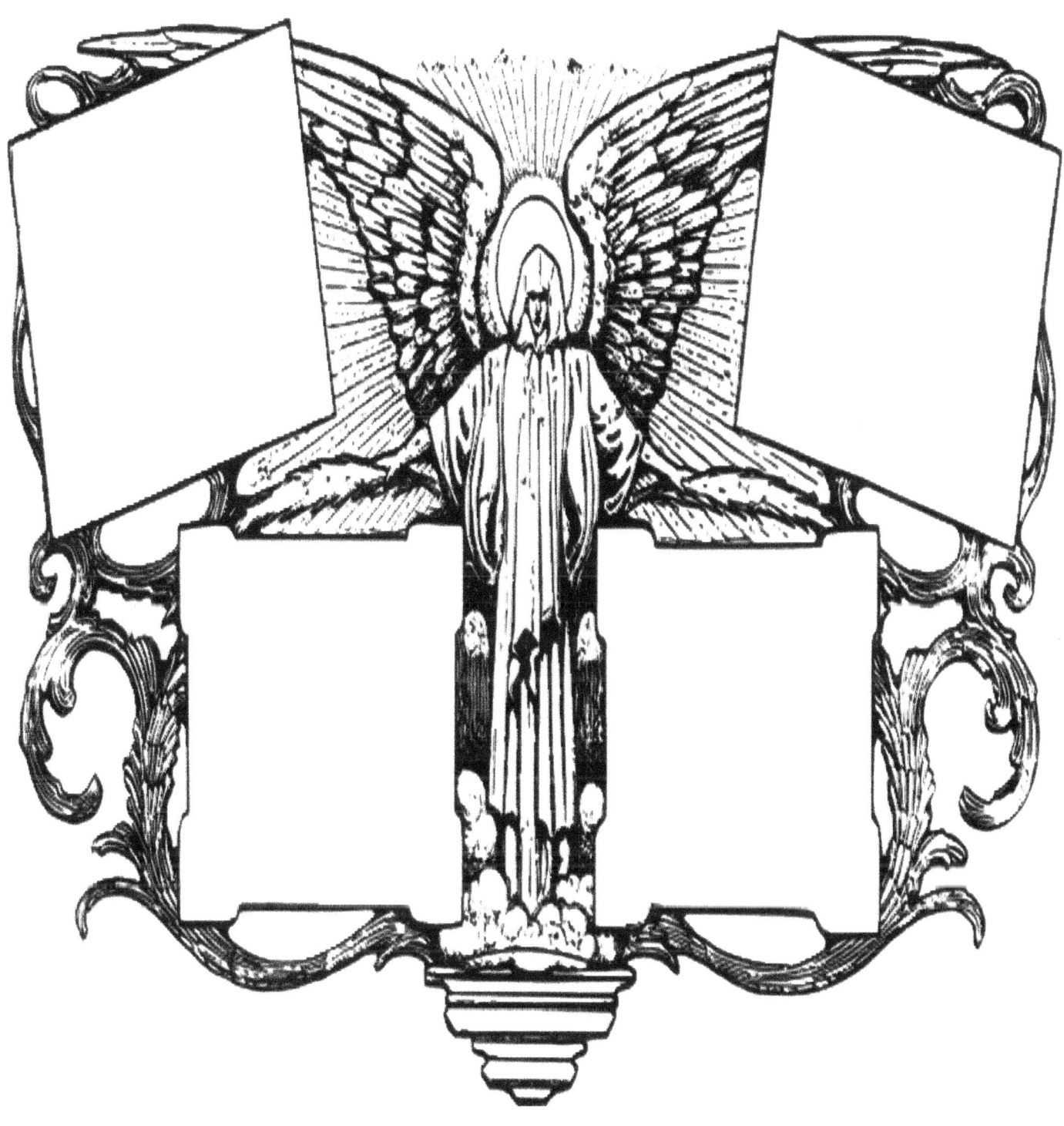

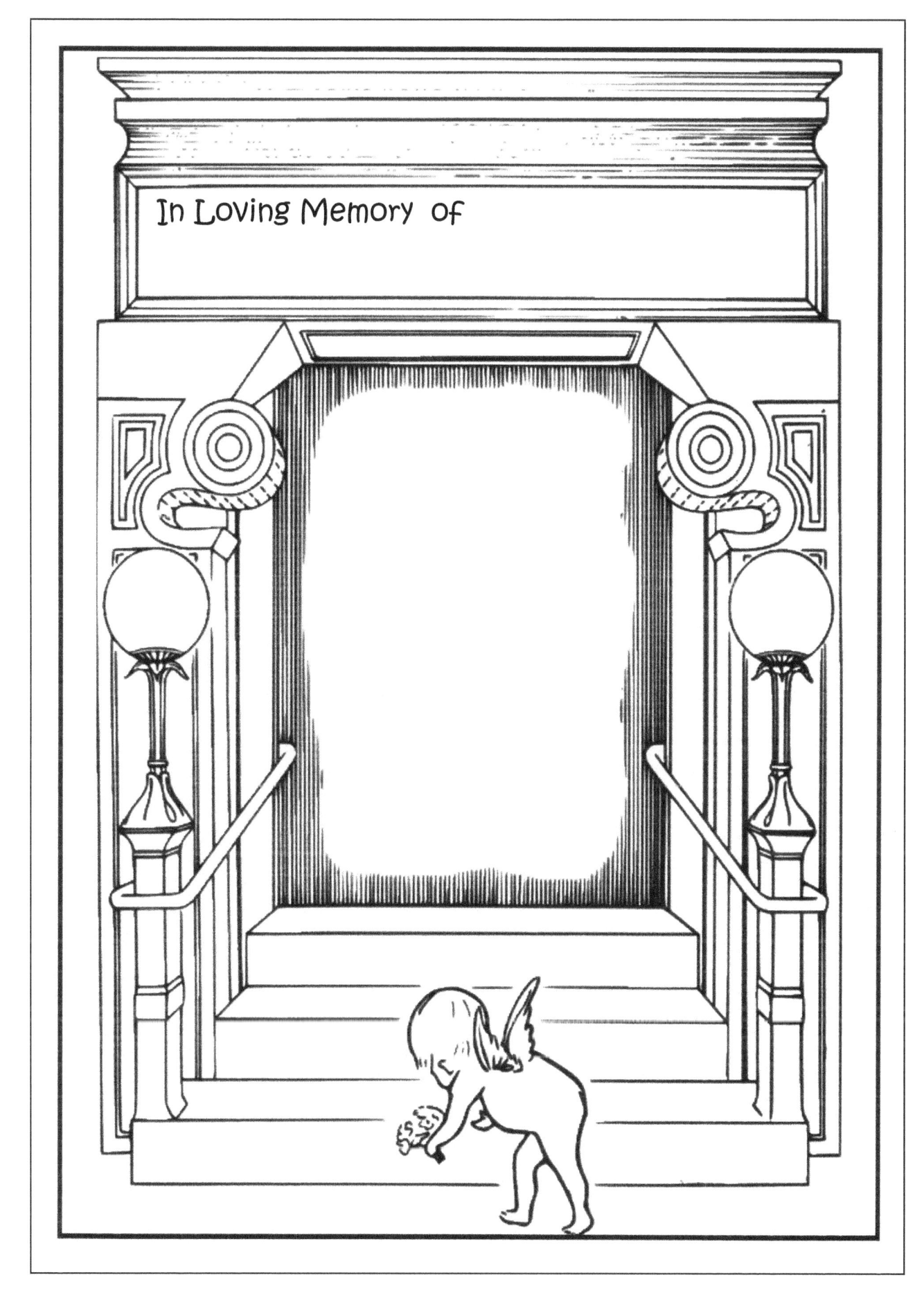

In Loving Memory of

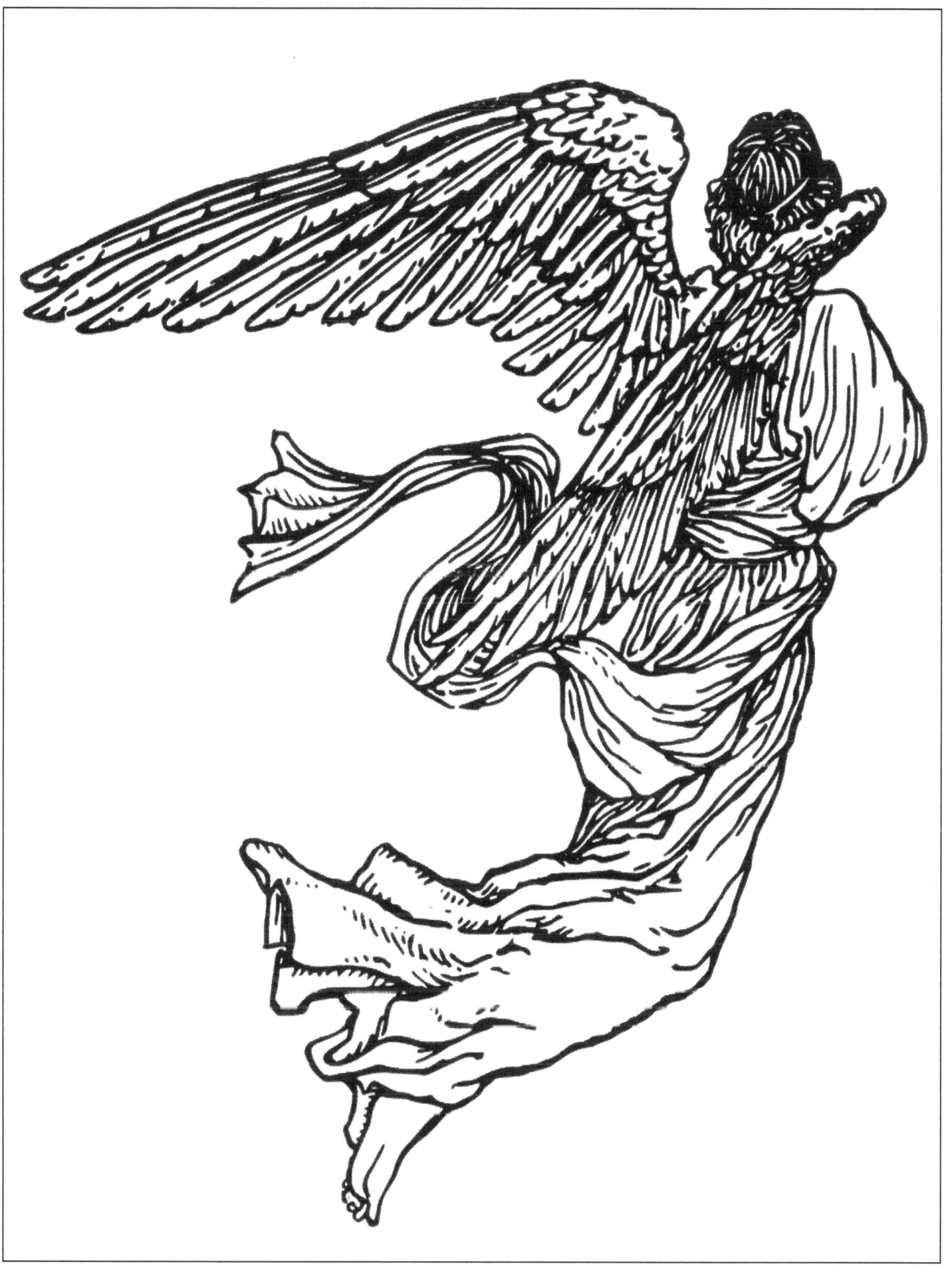

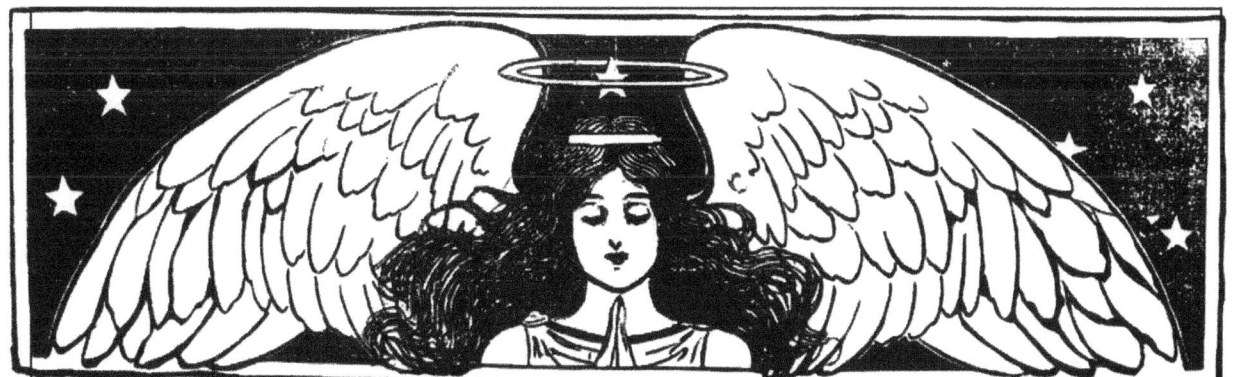

Cherished Moments

I love messages from the other side and know it was you when

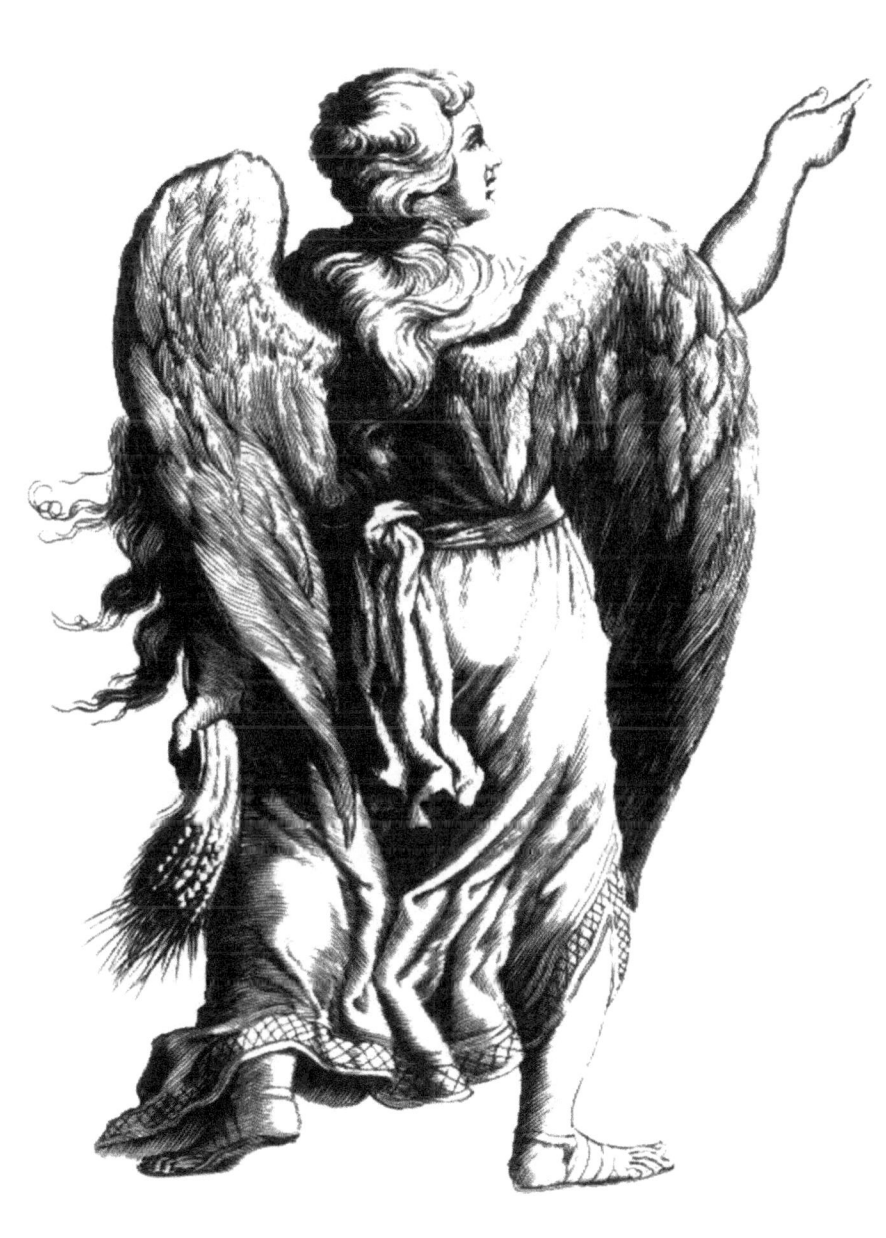

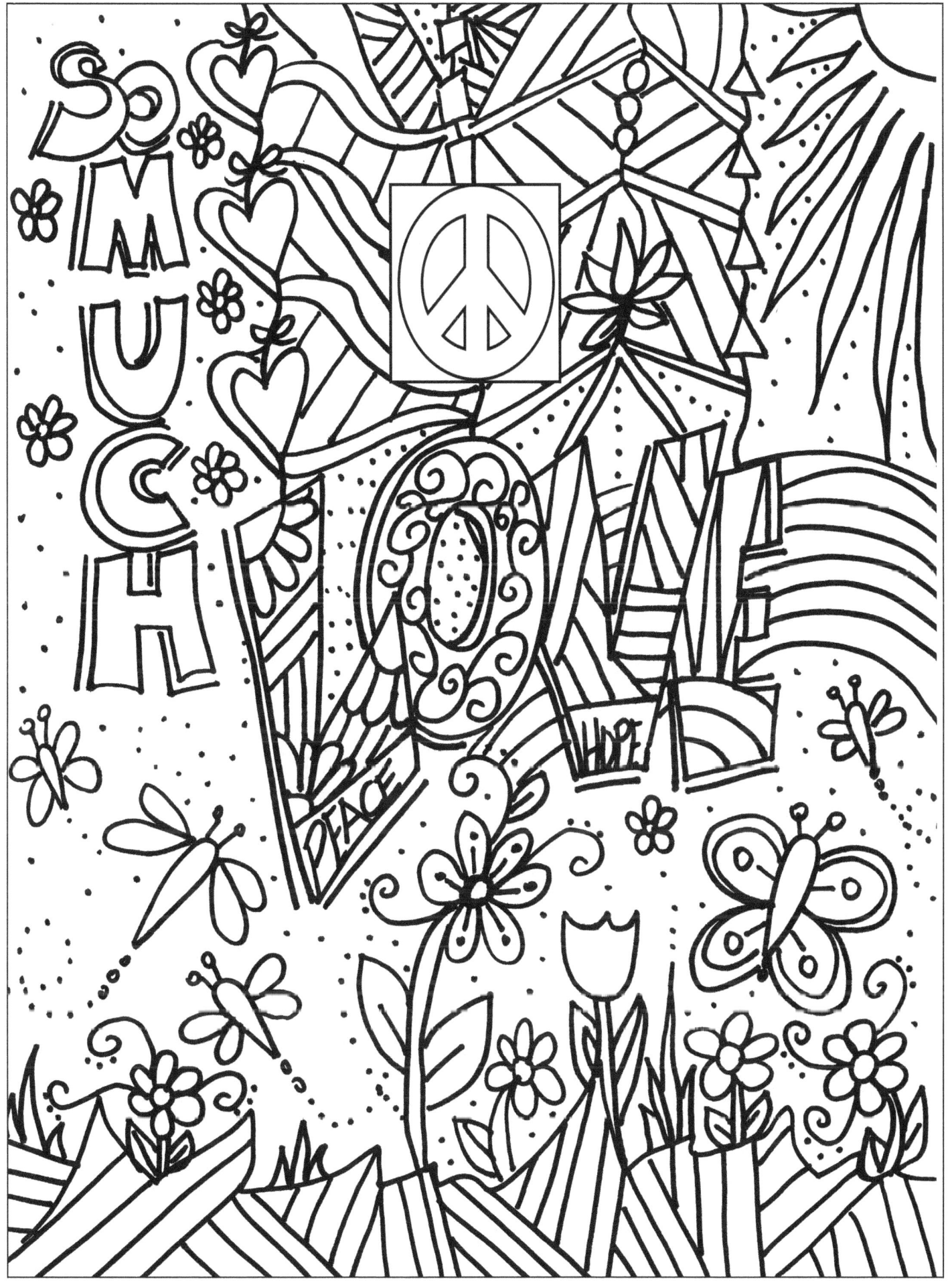

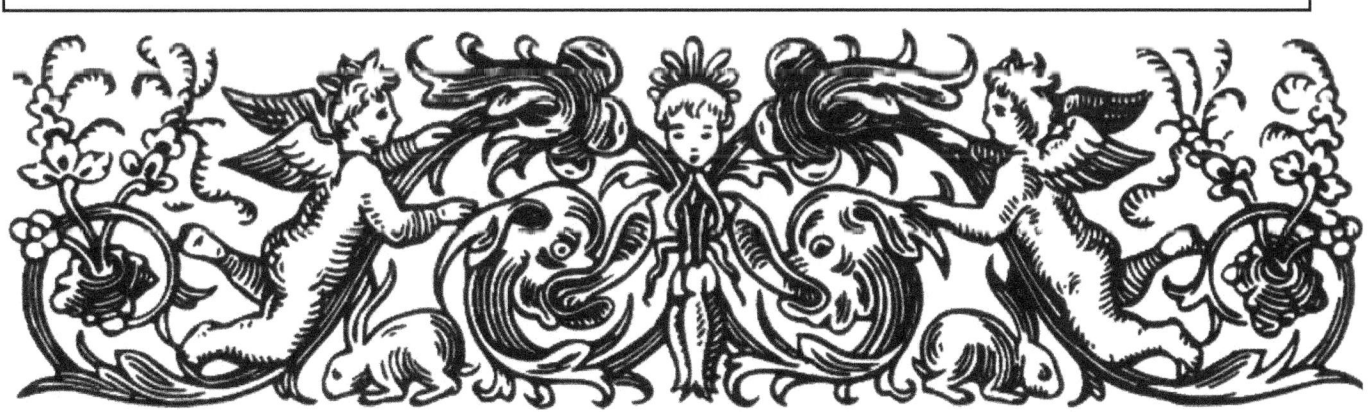

I loved the day when...

_____
_____
_____
_____
_____
_____
_____
_____
_____
_____
_____
_____
_____
_____
_____

"I am a thousand winds that blow.

I am the diamond glints on snow.

I am the sunlight on ripened grain.

I am the gentle autumn rain.

When you awaken in the morning's hush

I am the swift uplifting rush

of quiet birds in circled flight.

I am the soft star that shines at night."

~Mary Elizabeth Frye, 1932

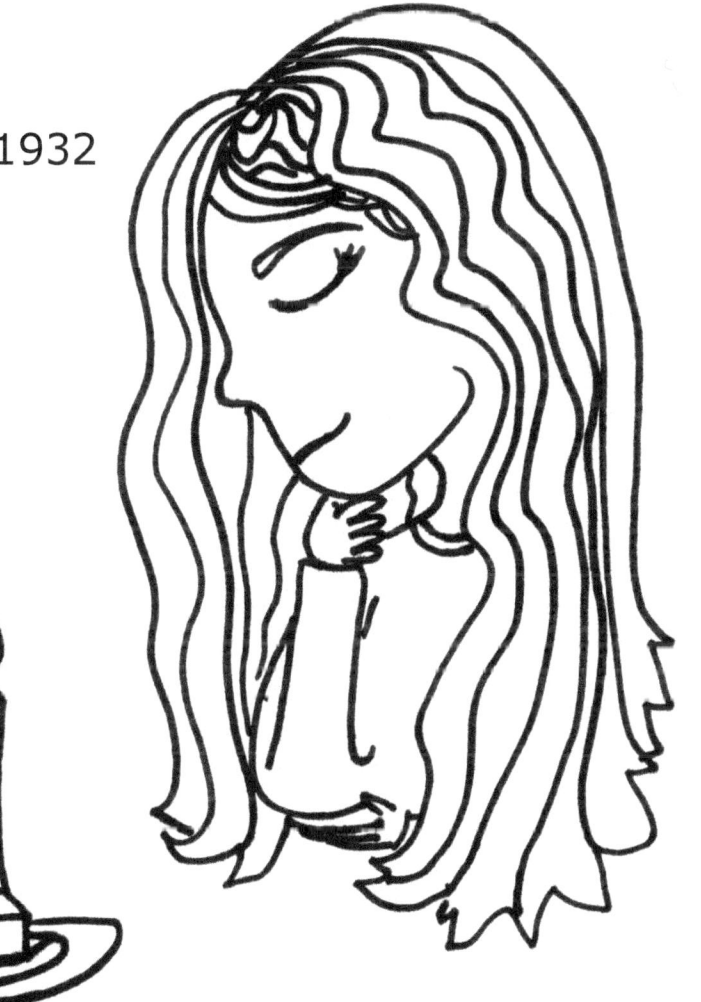

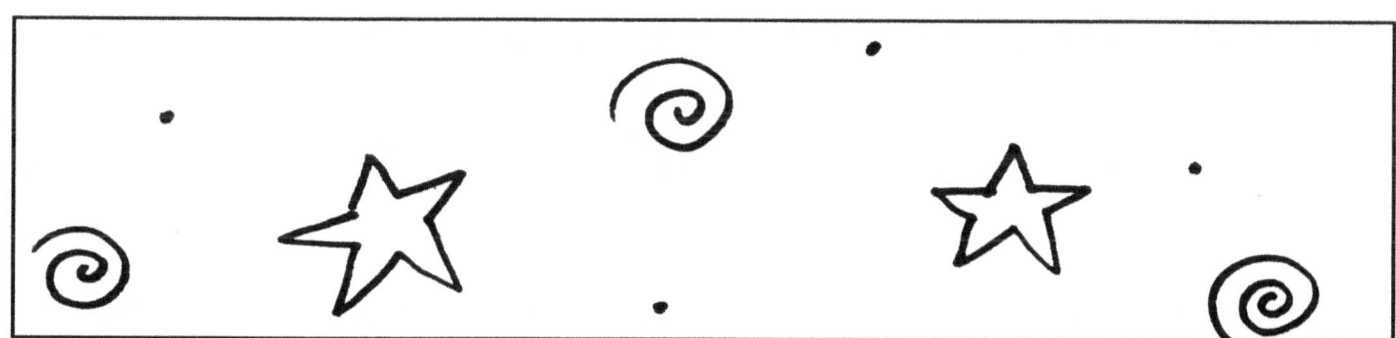

I will never forget...

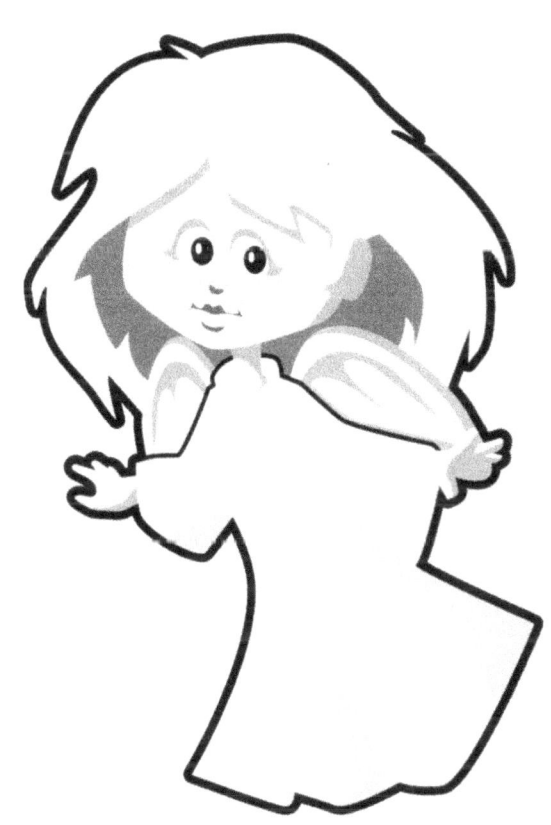

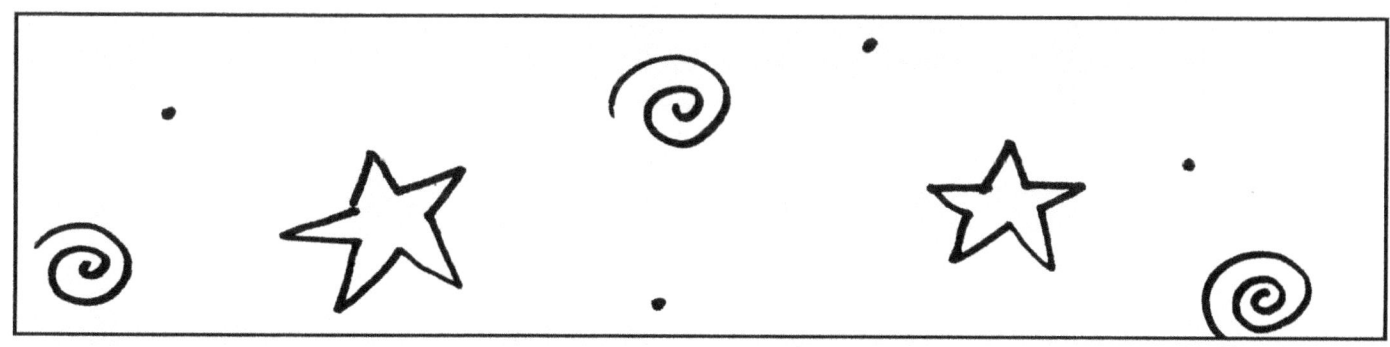

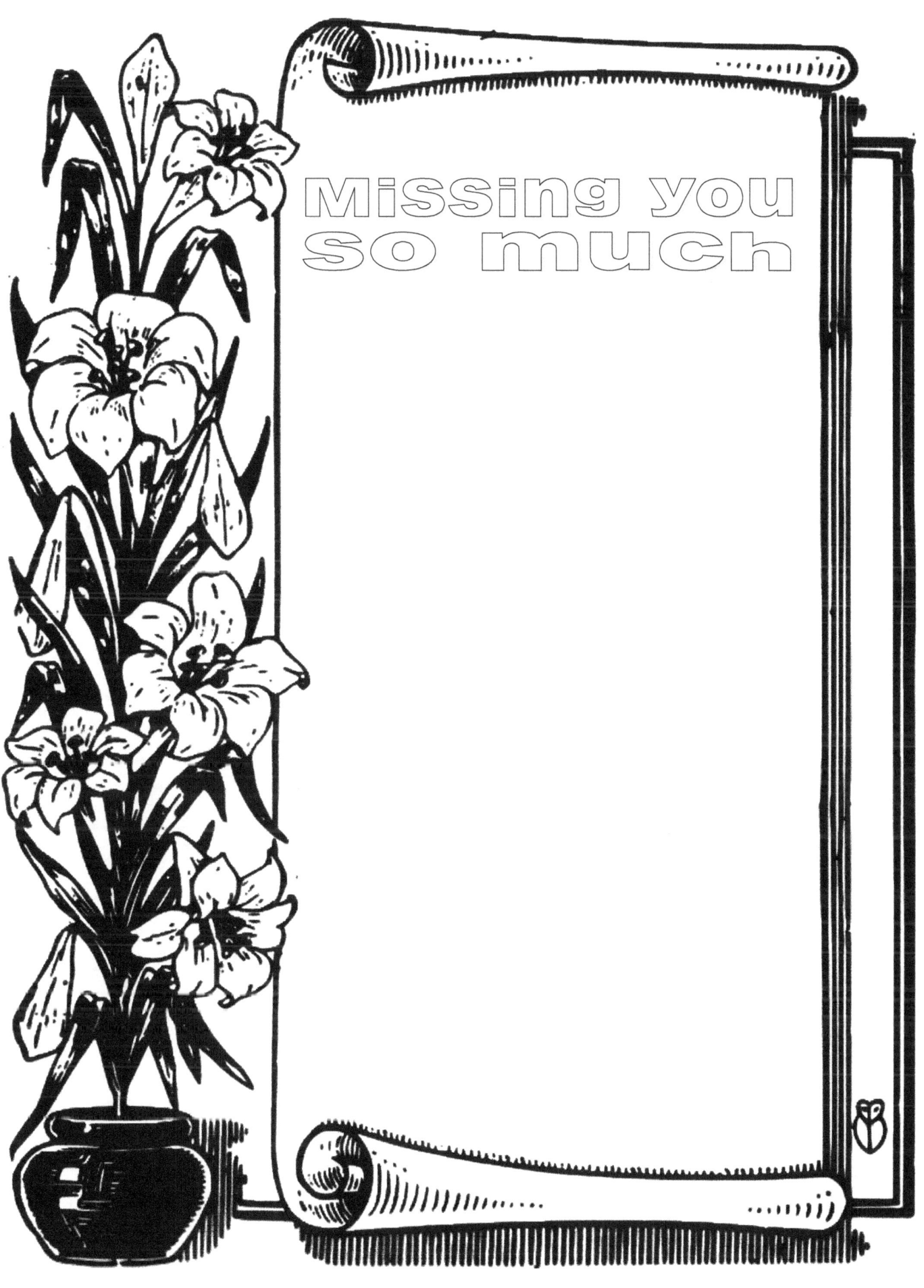

Missing you
so much

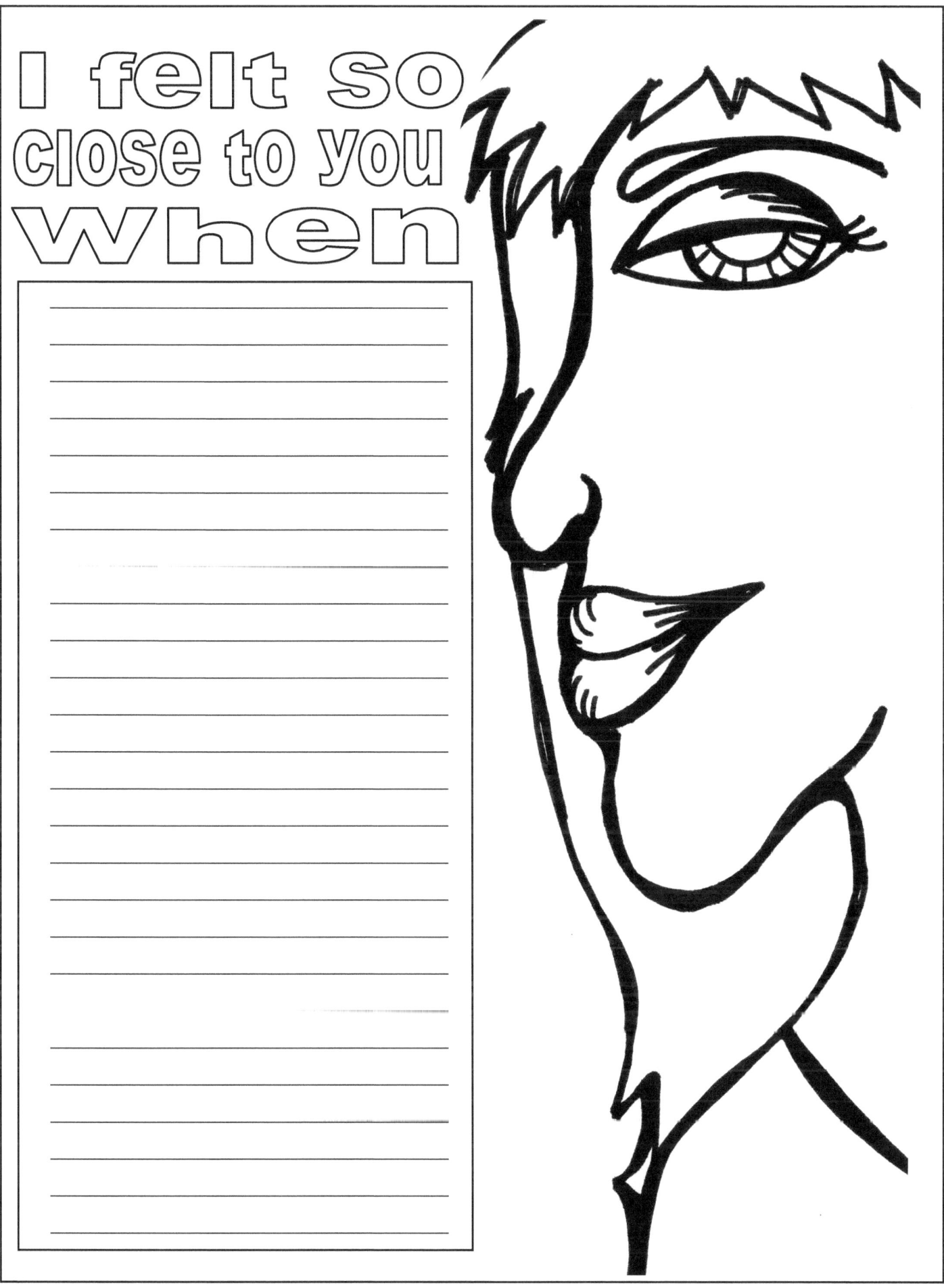

I felt so close to you when

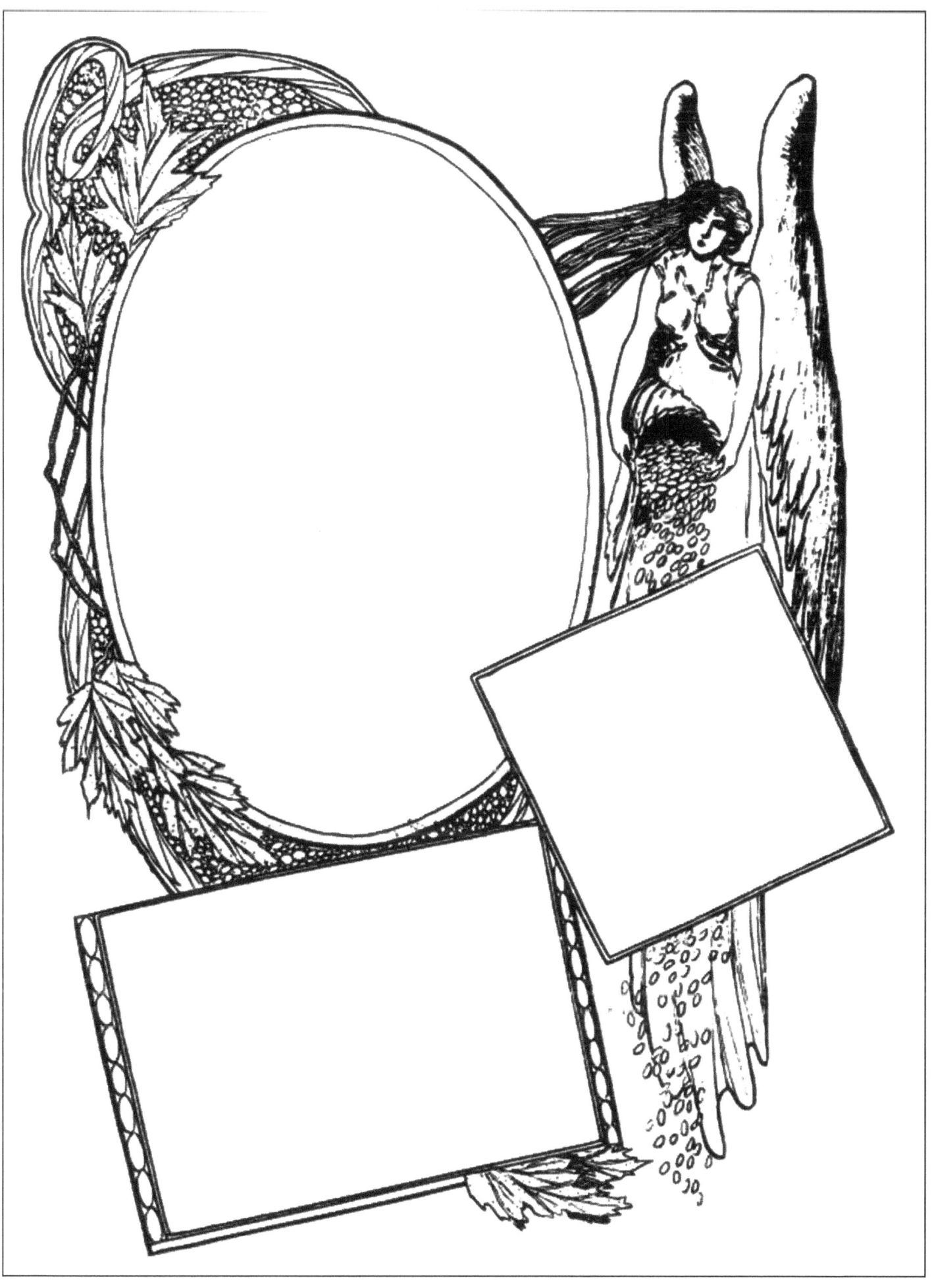

I can't believe you're gone

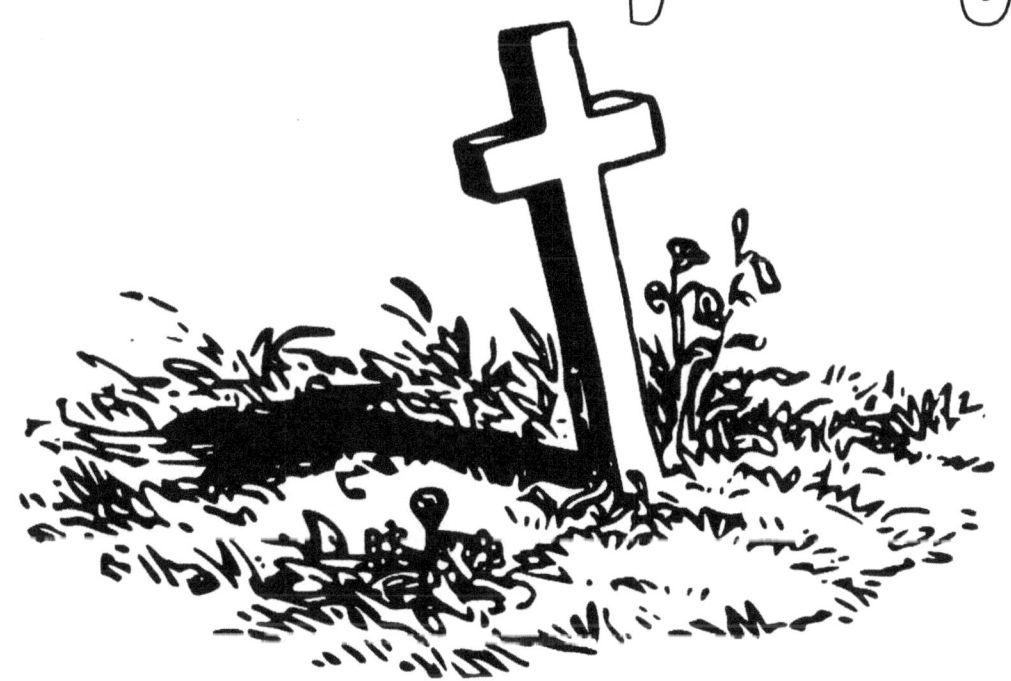

This Stage of Grief

_____
_____
_____
_____
_____
_____
_____
_____
_____
_____
_____
_____
_____
_____
_____
_____

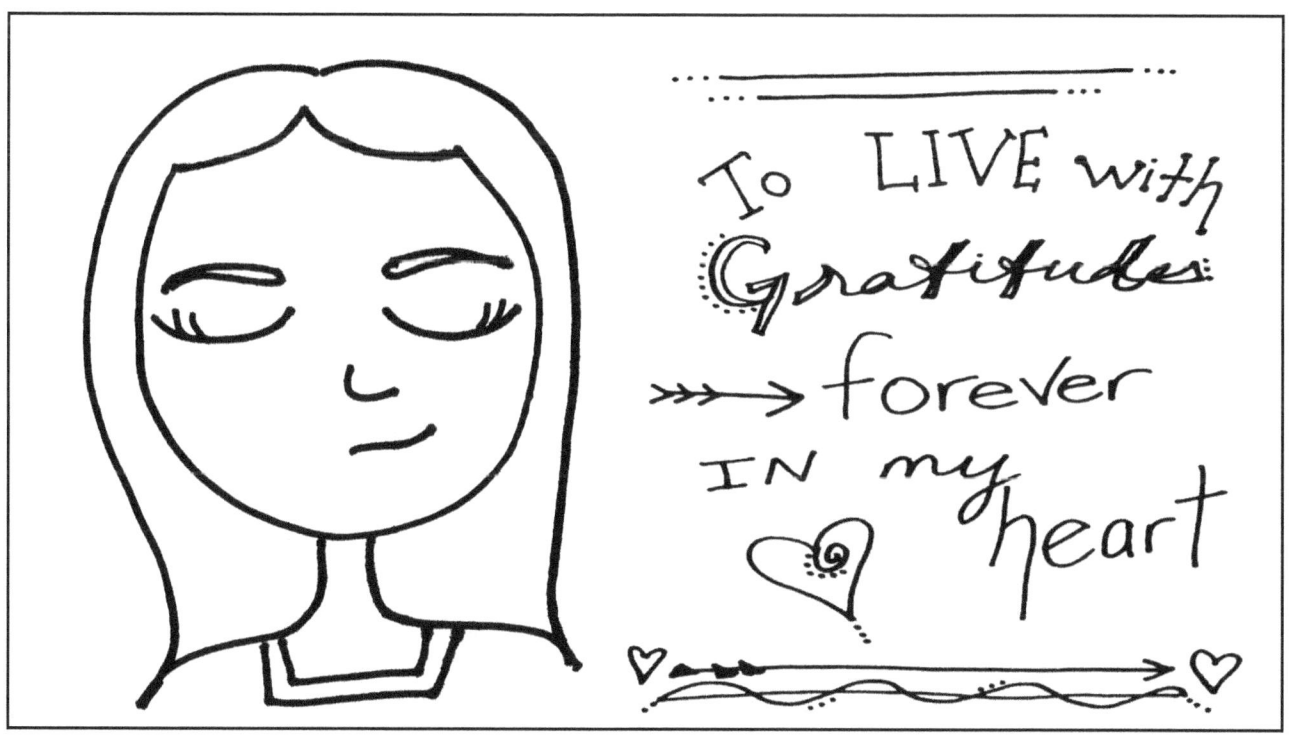

Thank you for sharing your life with me. I miss you so much and wish you were here right now so I could look into your eyes and tell you....

Be in peace my love

Parting is such sweet sorrow

~Shakespeare, Romeo & Juliet

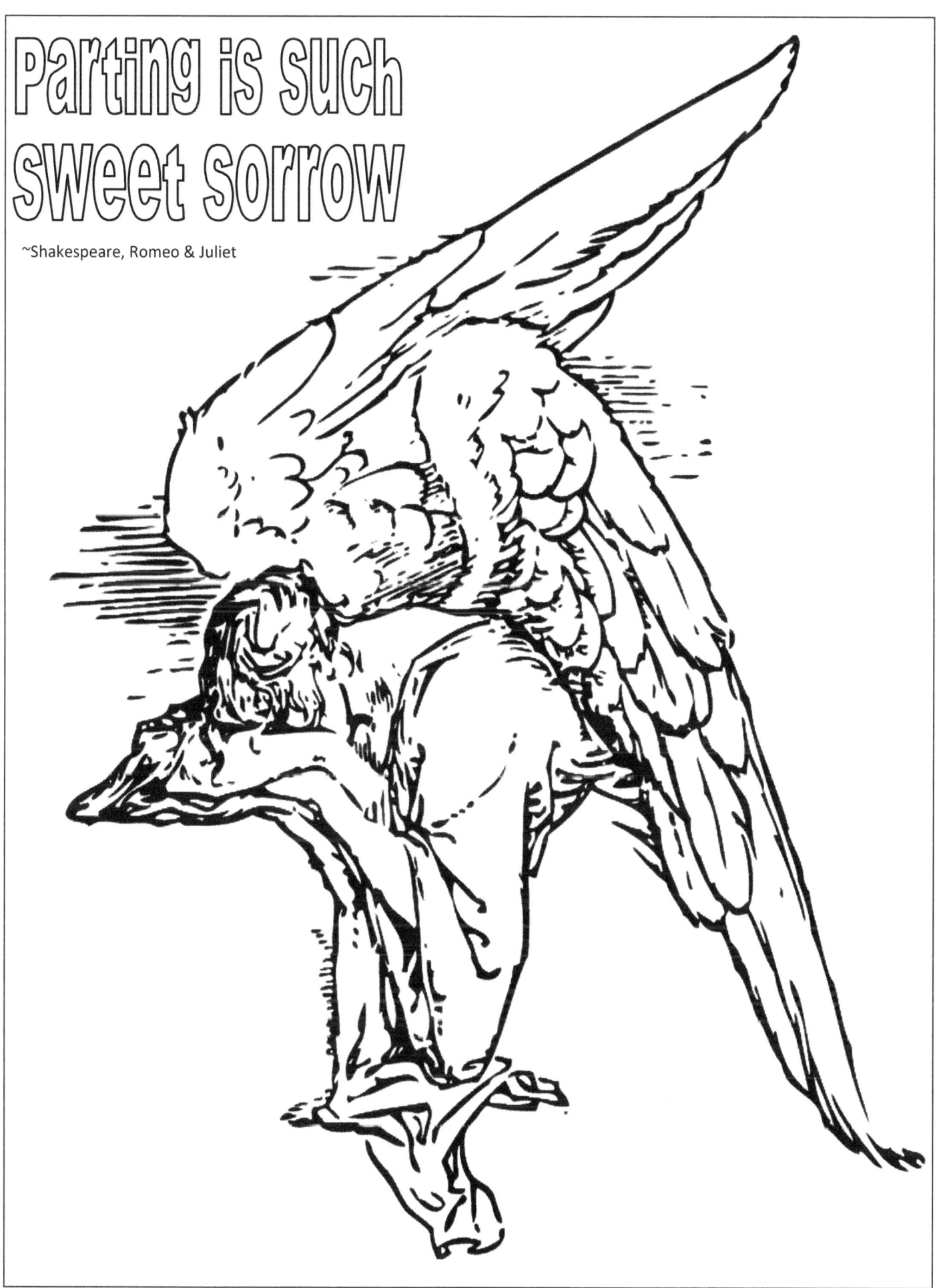

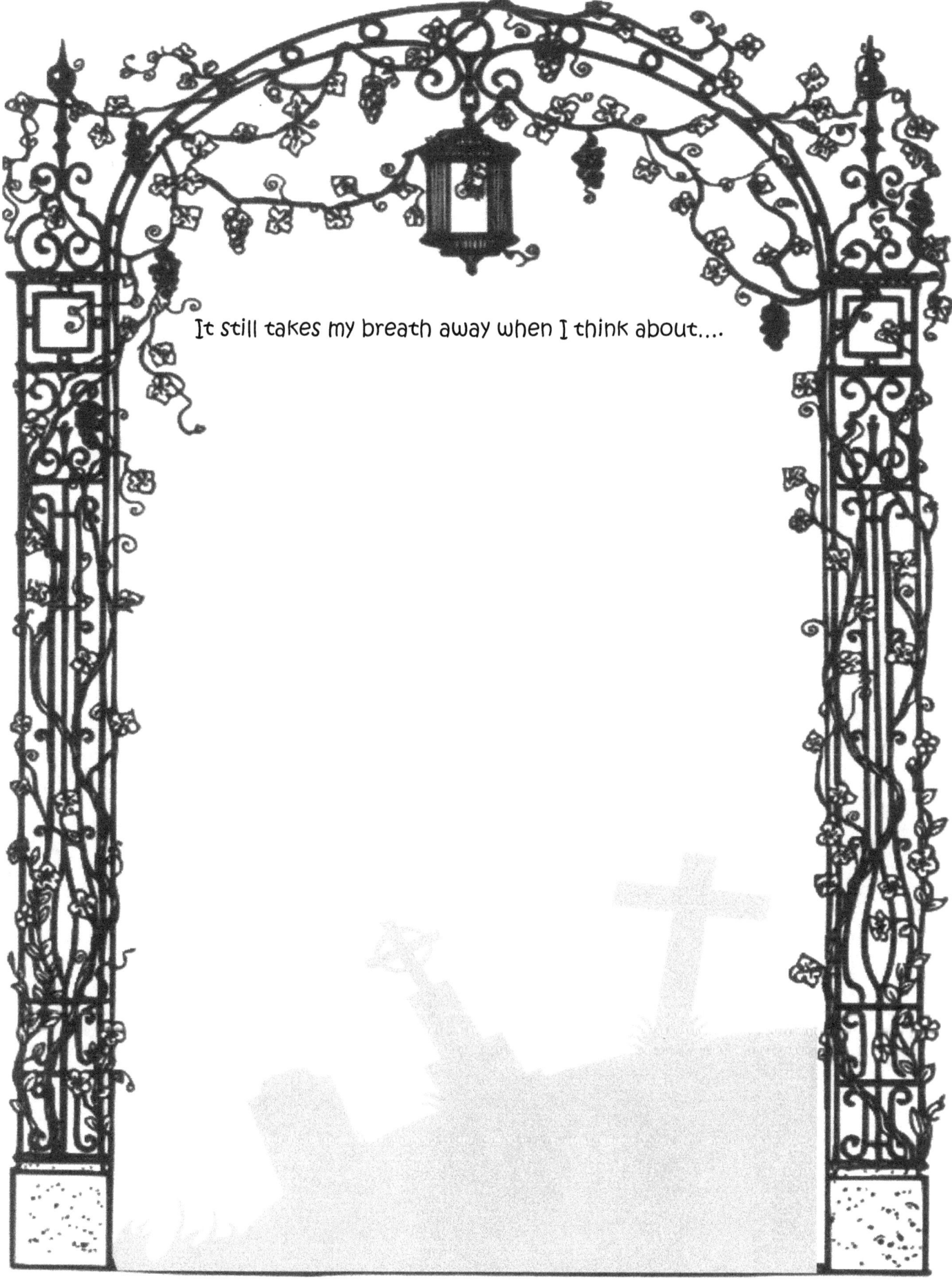

It still takes my breath away when I think about....

I feel such an emptiness
Life will never be
the same
Without you

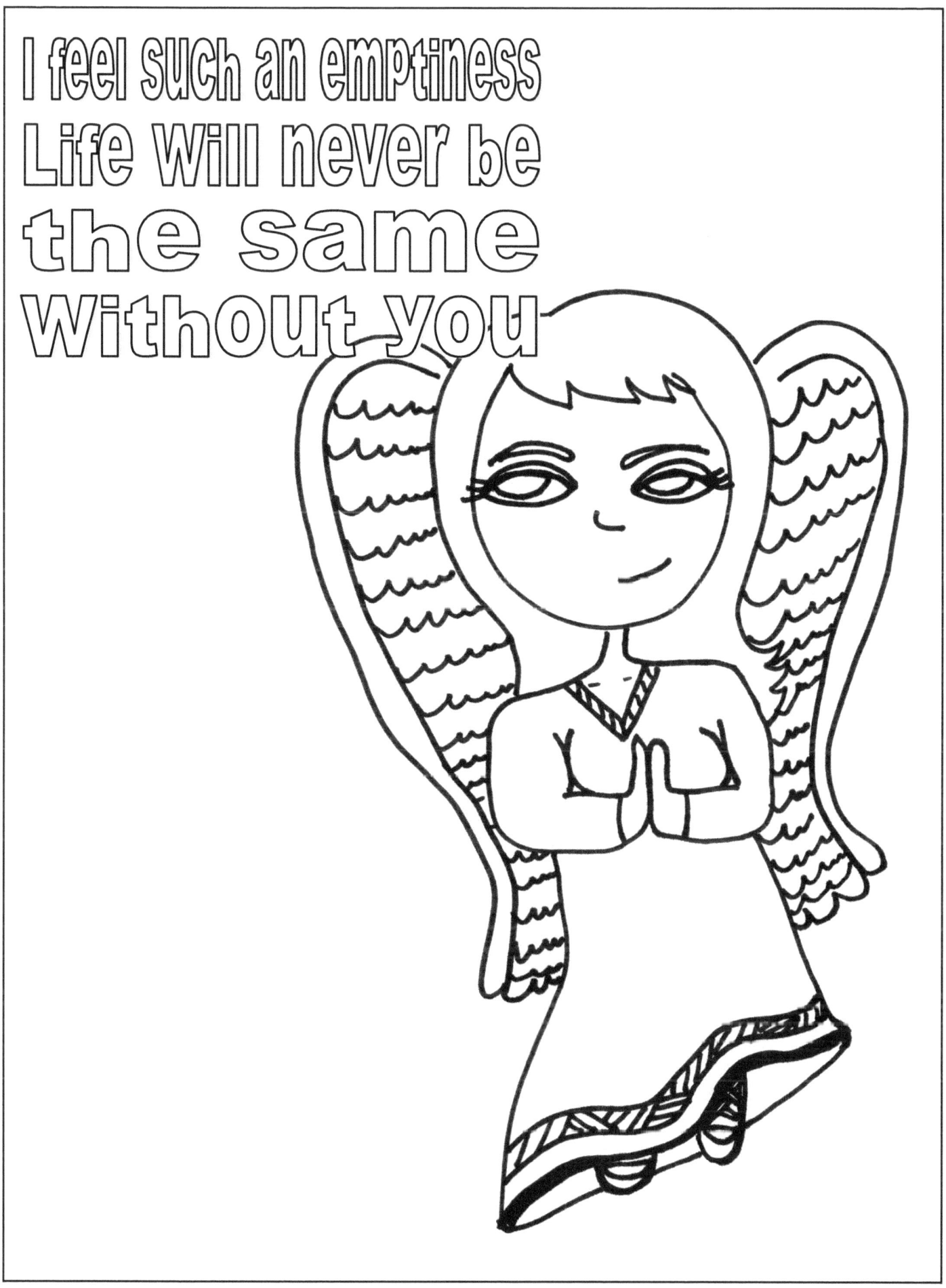

Everything feels so raw. Being with others isn't helping. Being alone feels like too much. I'm having the hardest time admitting to and believing you are gone. I will not fight these feelings. This is one of those days that I will allow these feelings to work their way through me. As I live in this moment, through this stage of grief, breathing, working towards accepting the truth, I will honour your passing by....

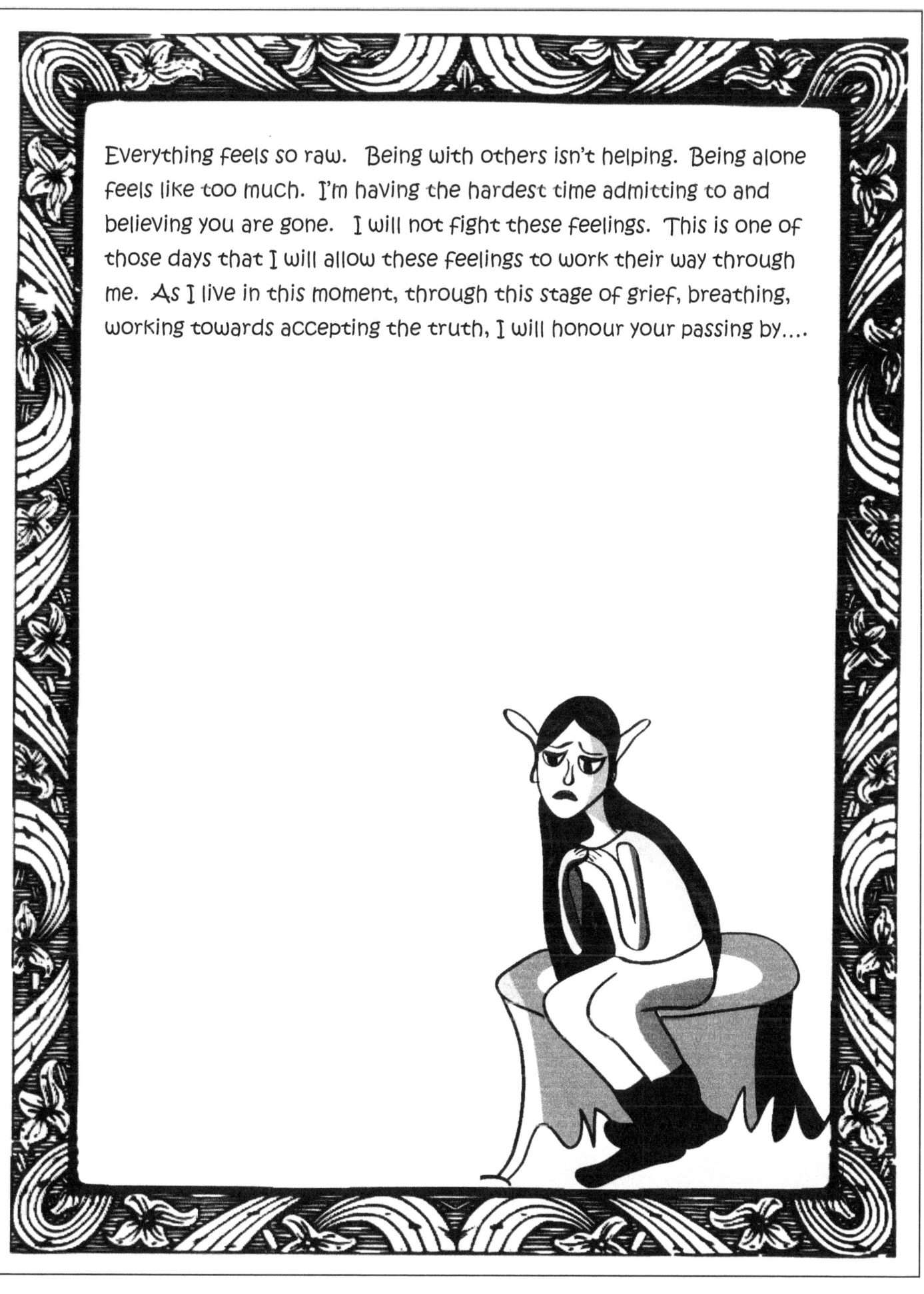

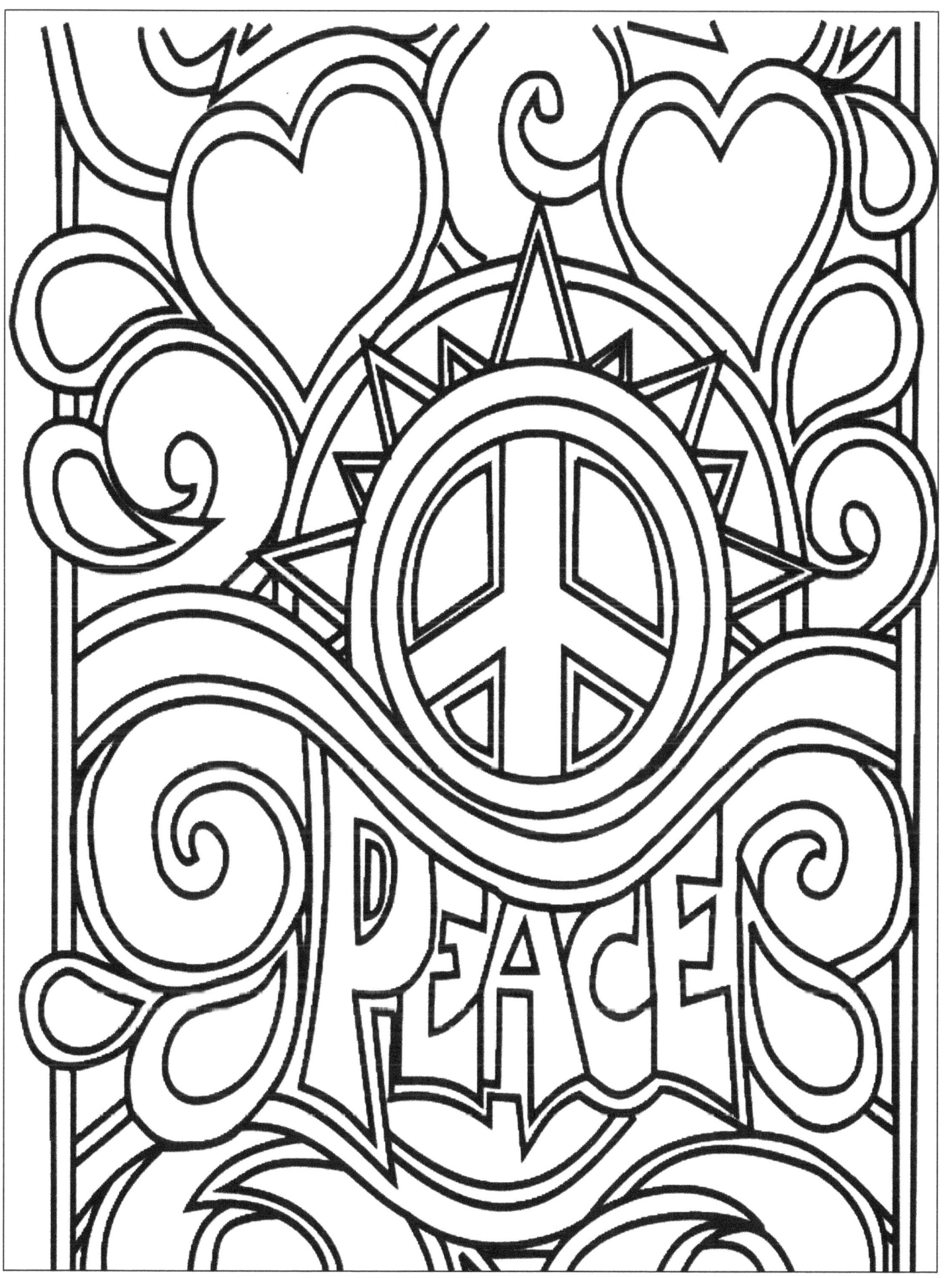

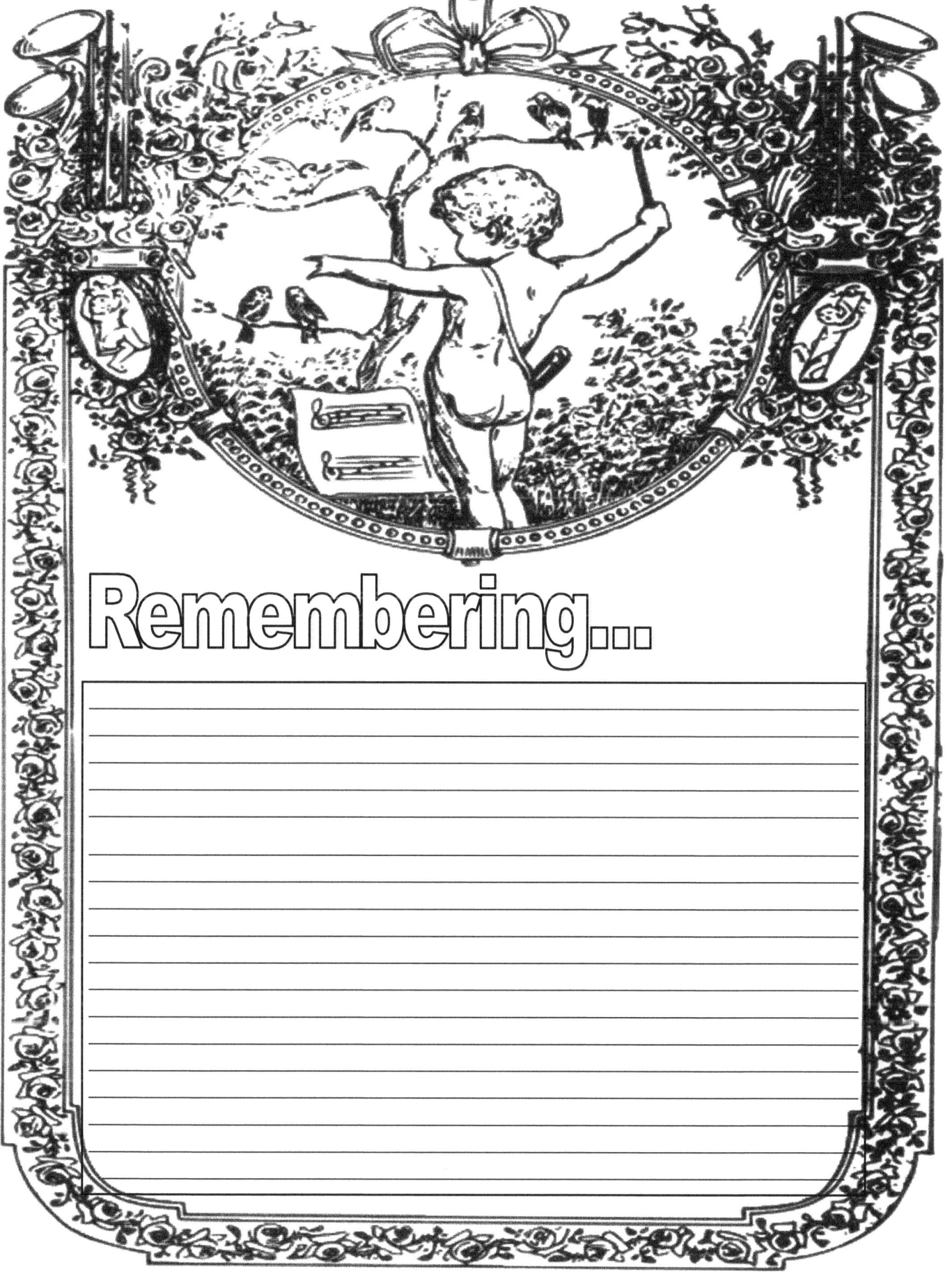

Remembering...

"May flights of angels sing thee to thy rest."
~Hamlet, Shakespeare

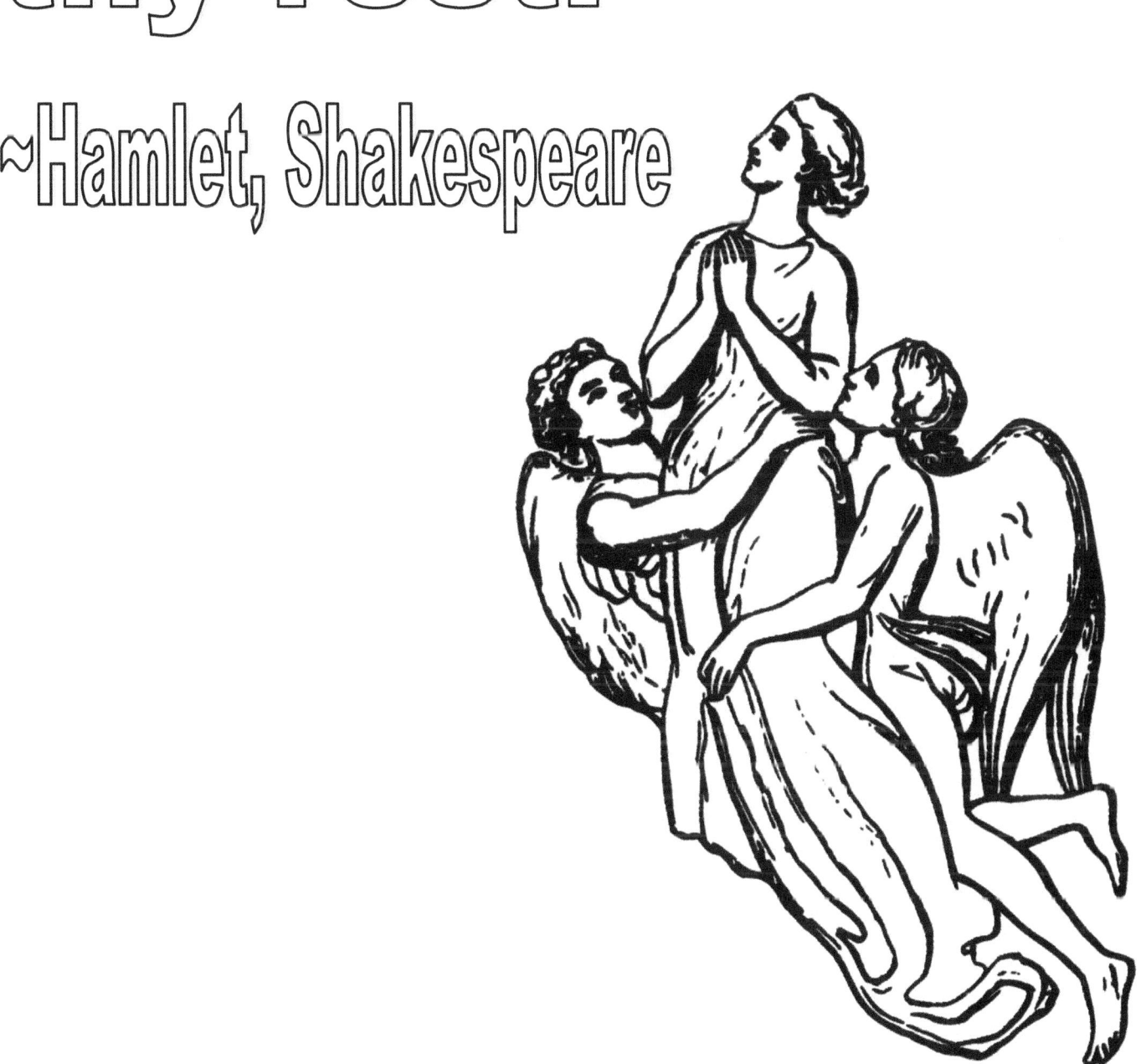

I can't even...

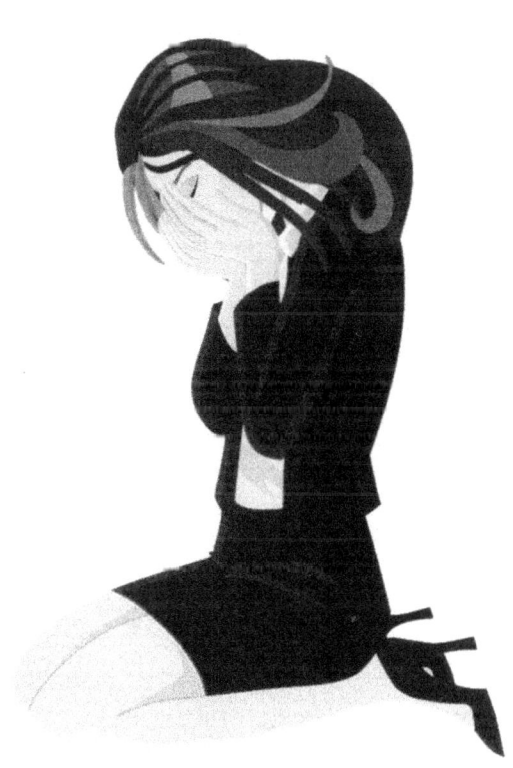

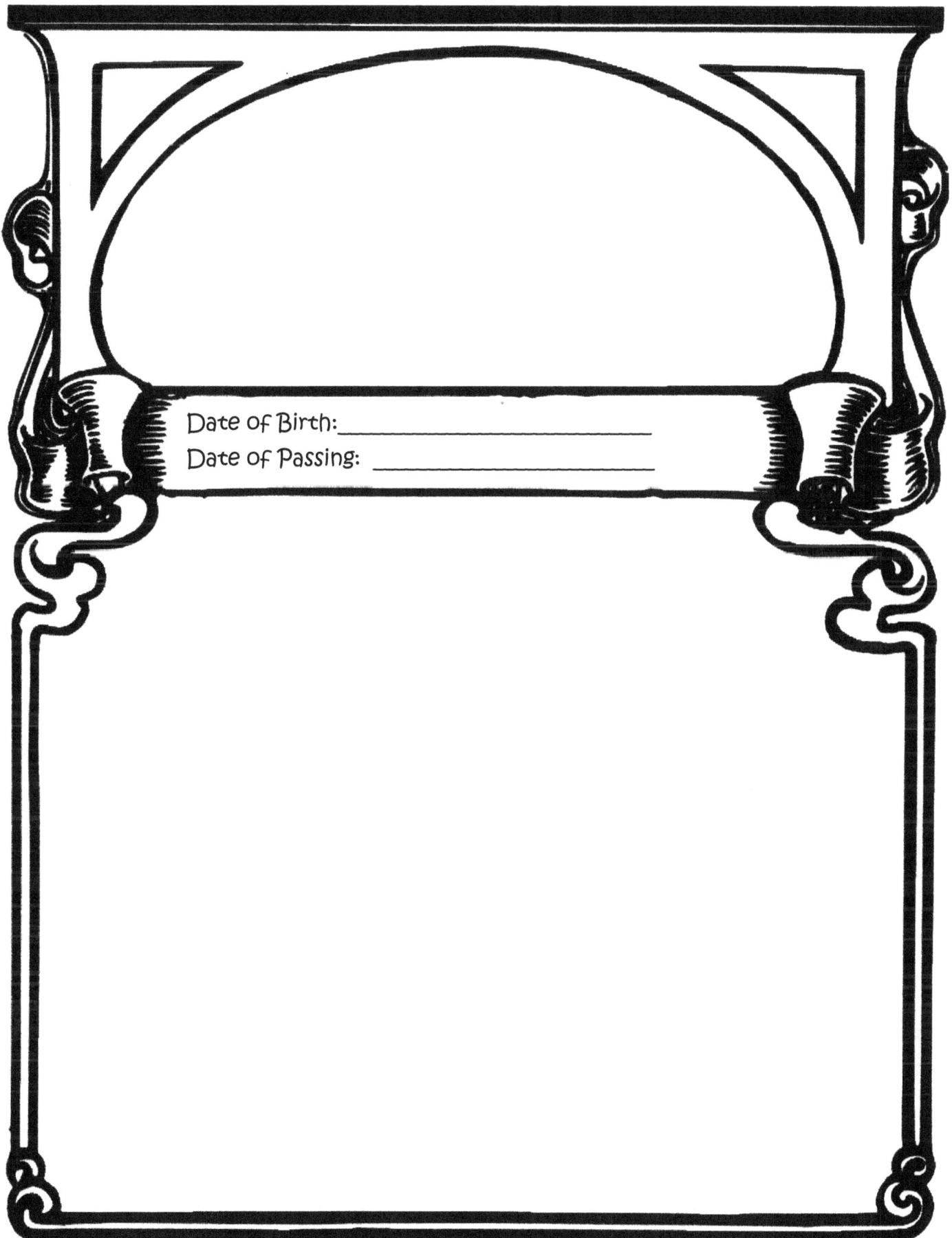

Date of Birth:_____

Date of Passing: _____

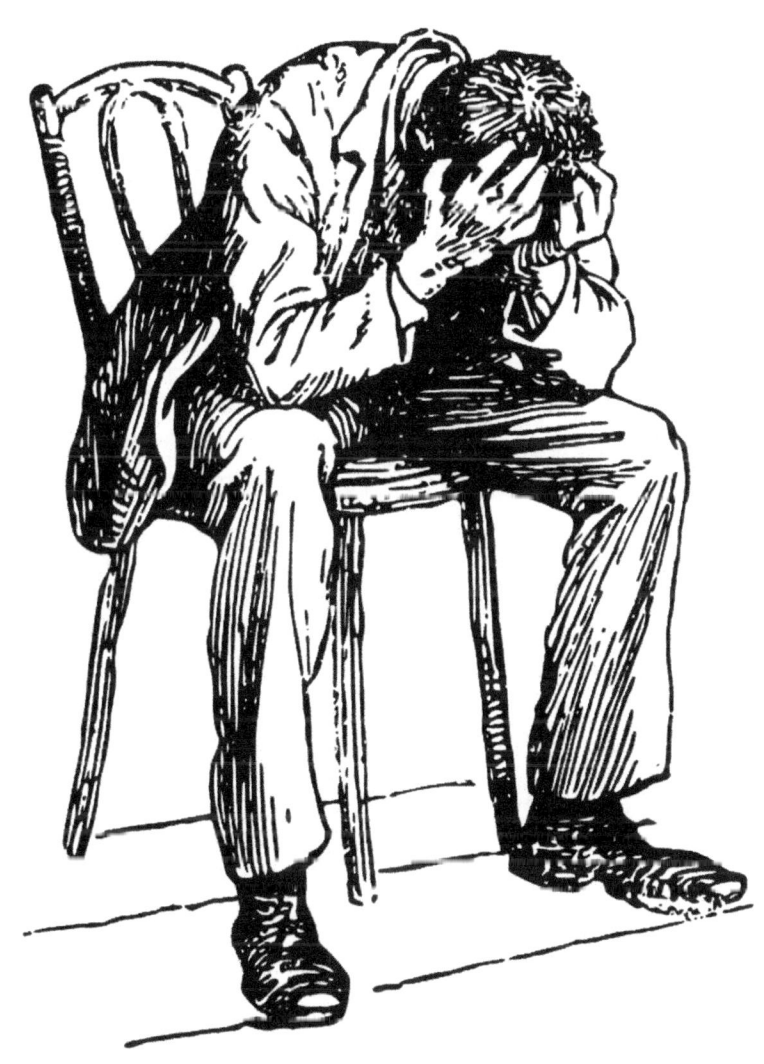

Such a challenging day

A great memory of you

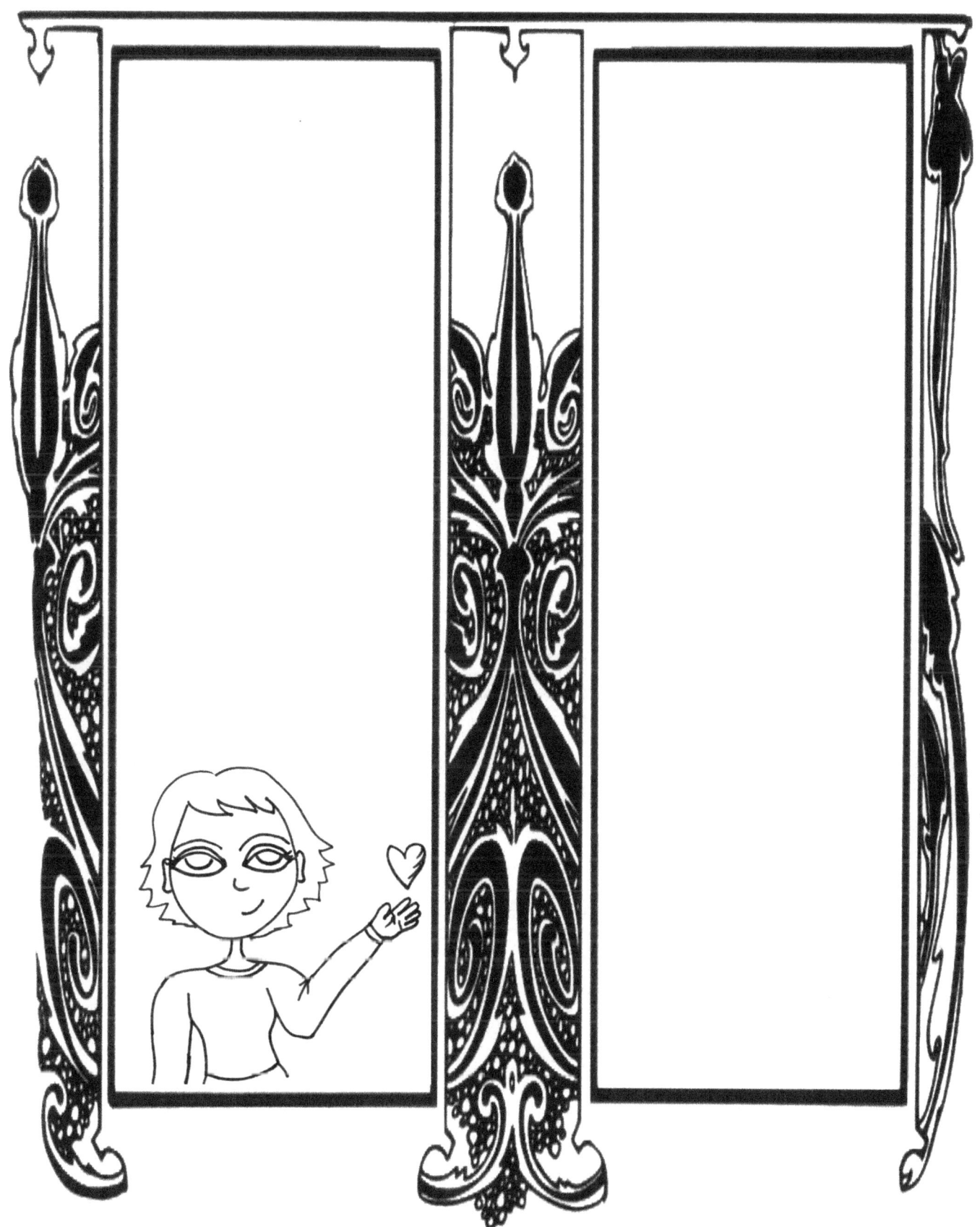

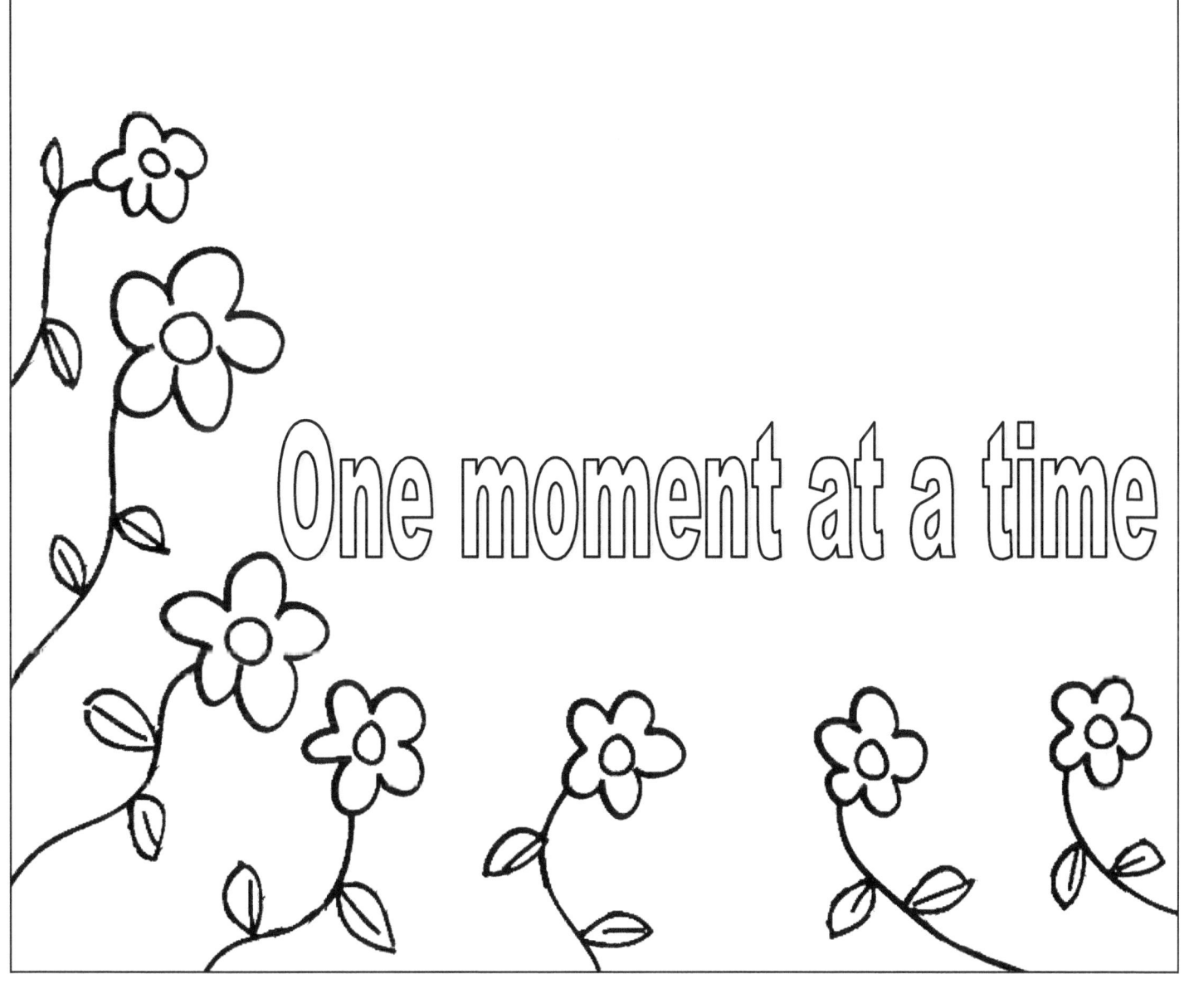

One moment at a time

The circle of life

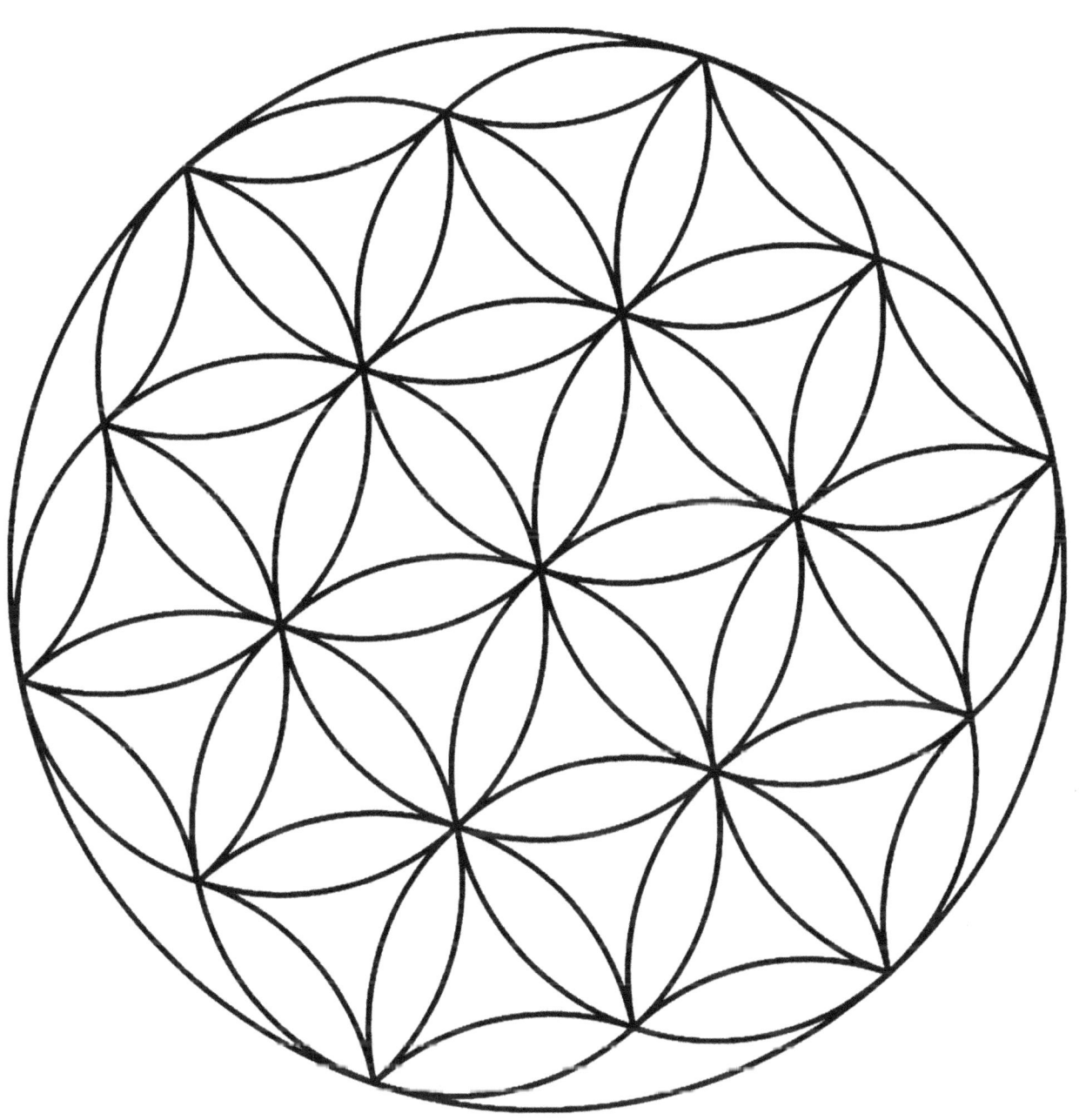

viewing the world with new eyes

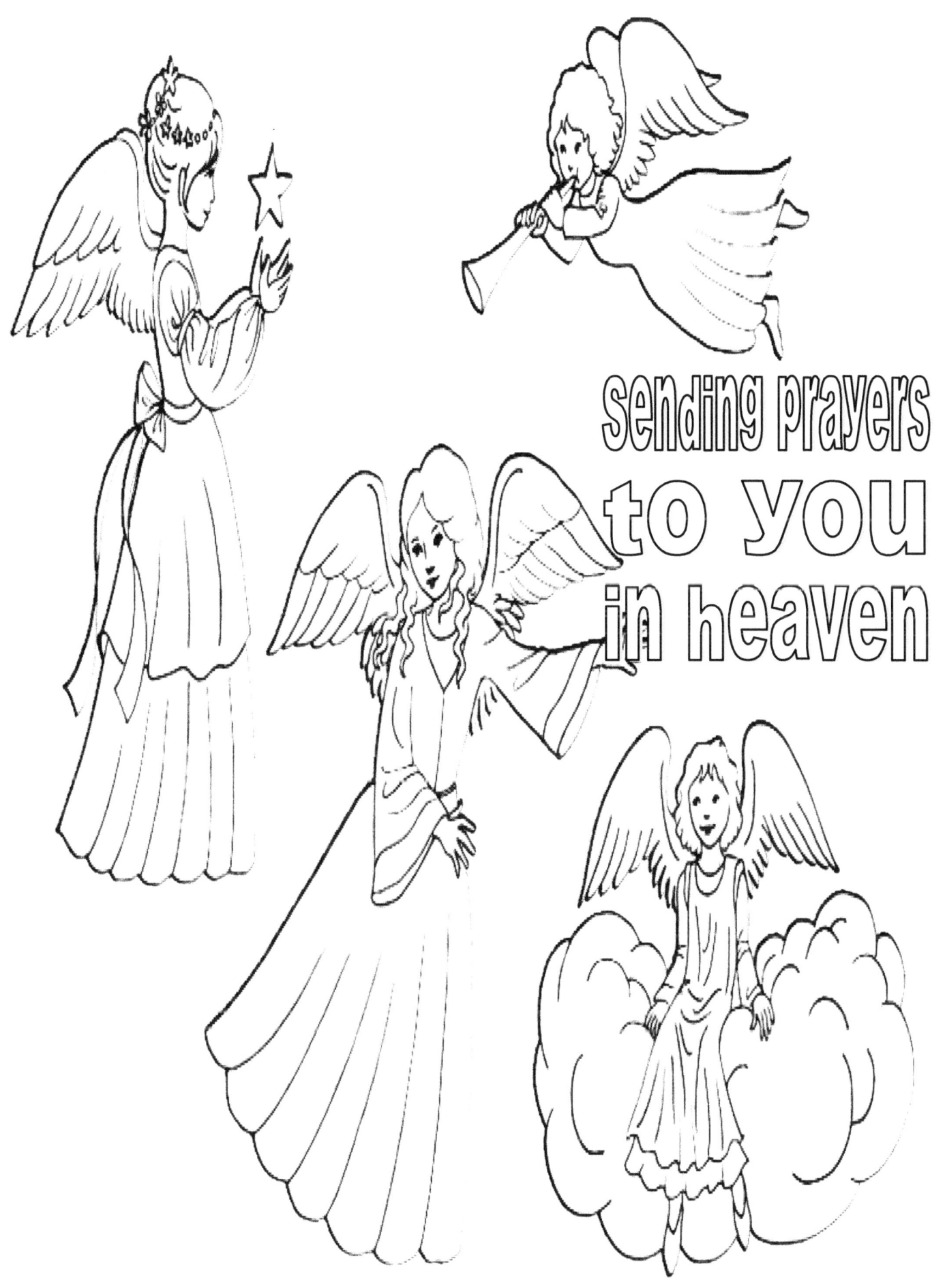

sending prayers
to you
in heaven

Holidays are hard
I will honour you
& the new normal
each holiday by

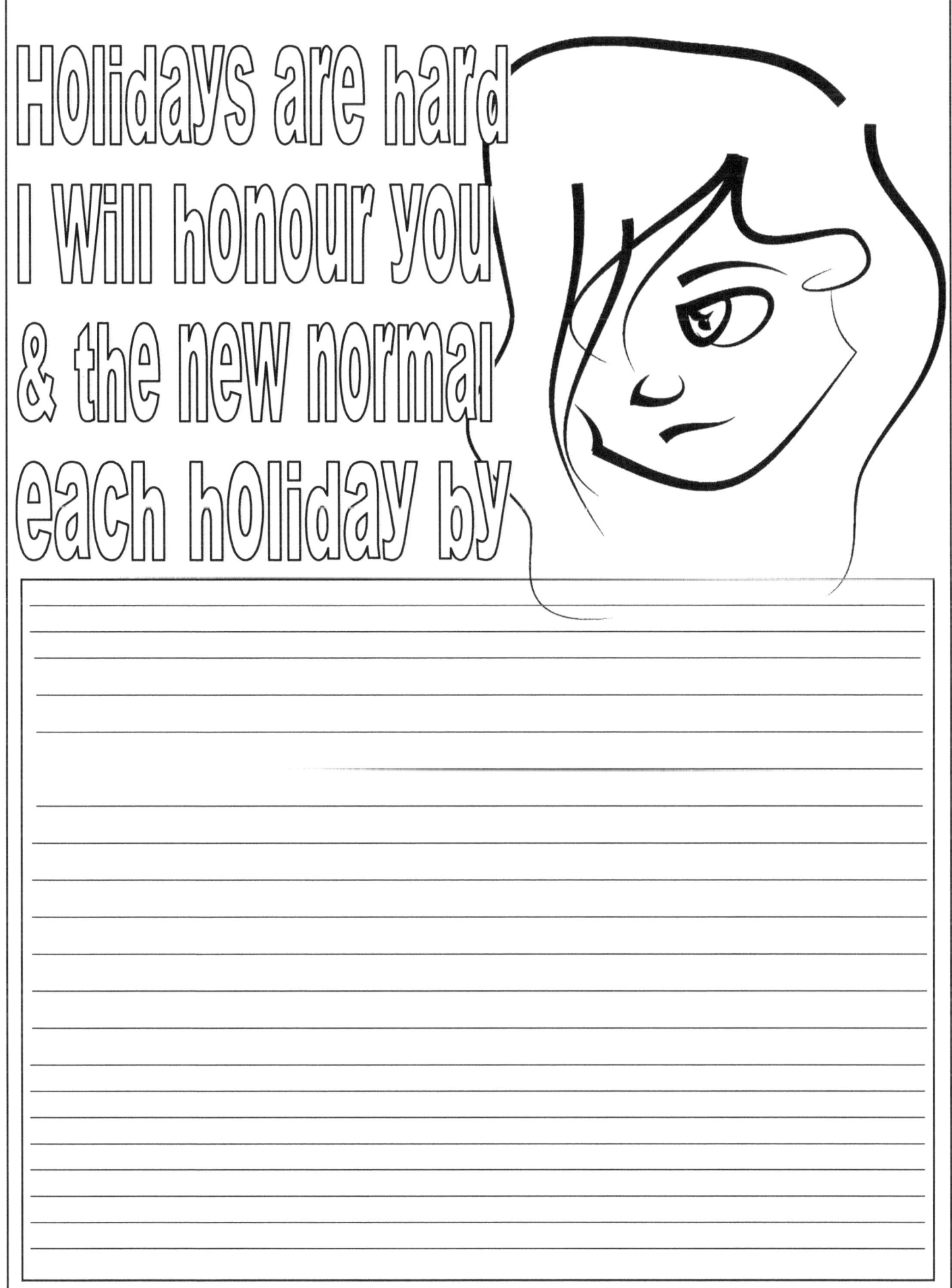

Our story is not over

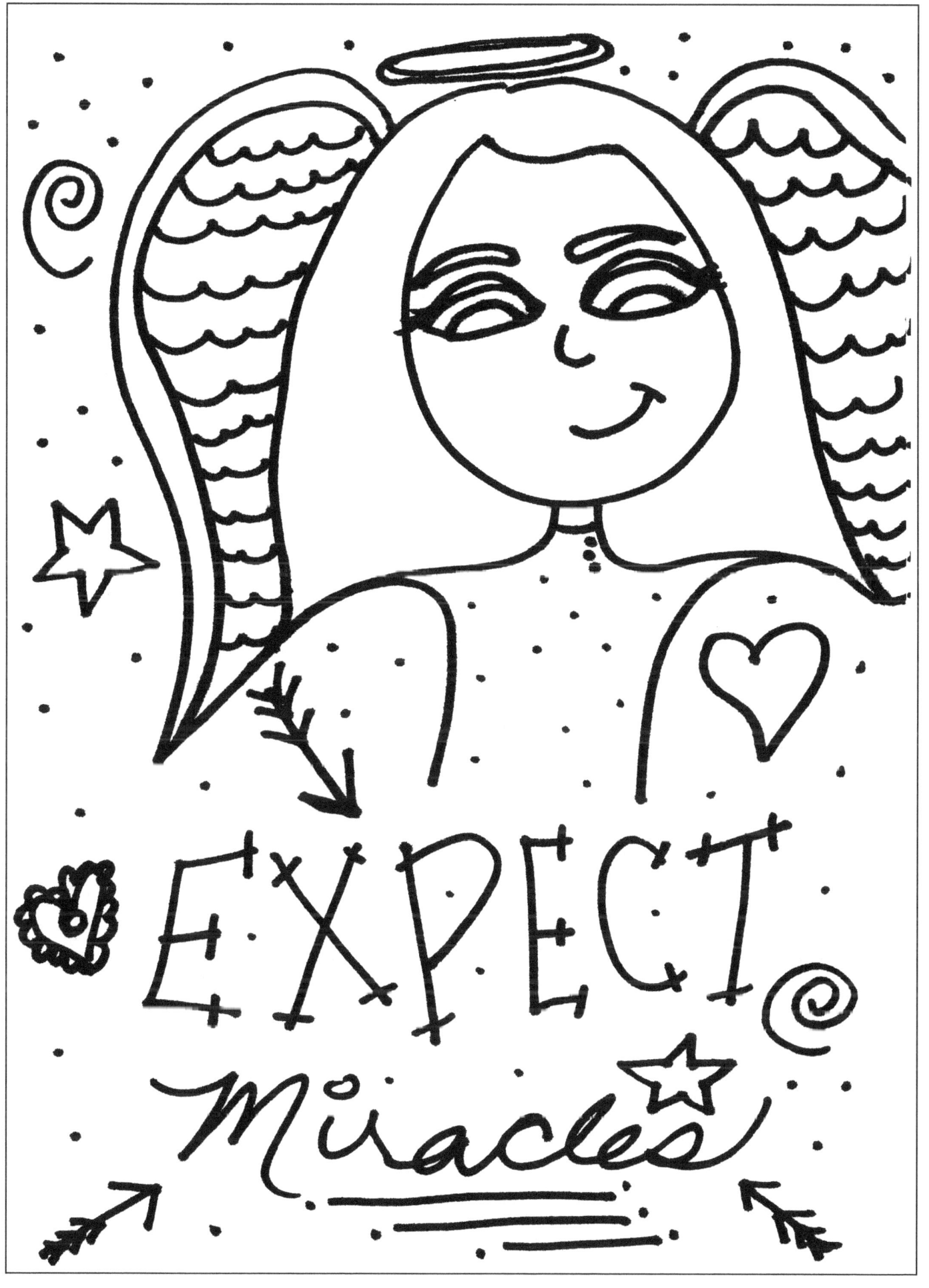

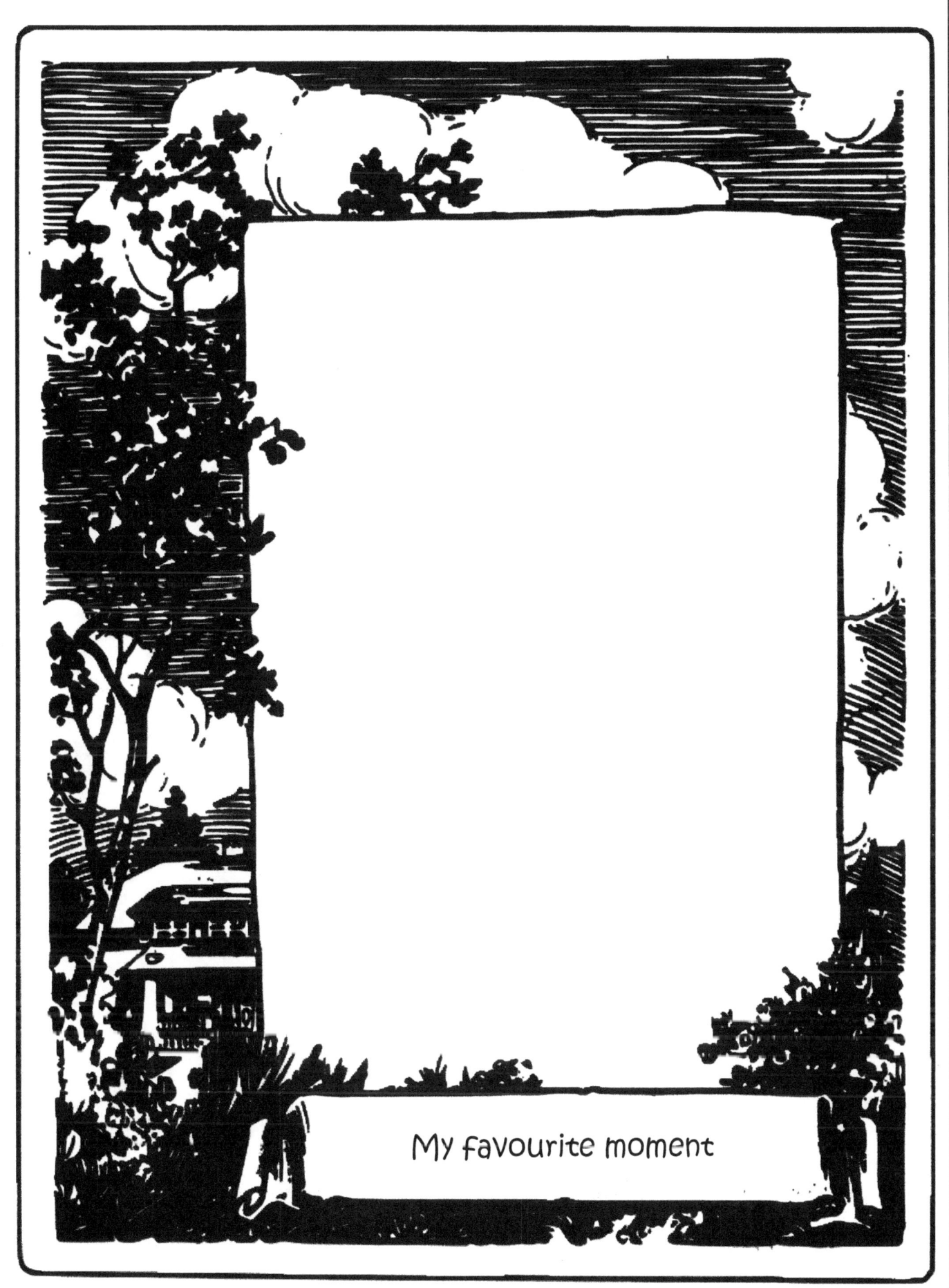

My favourite moment

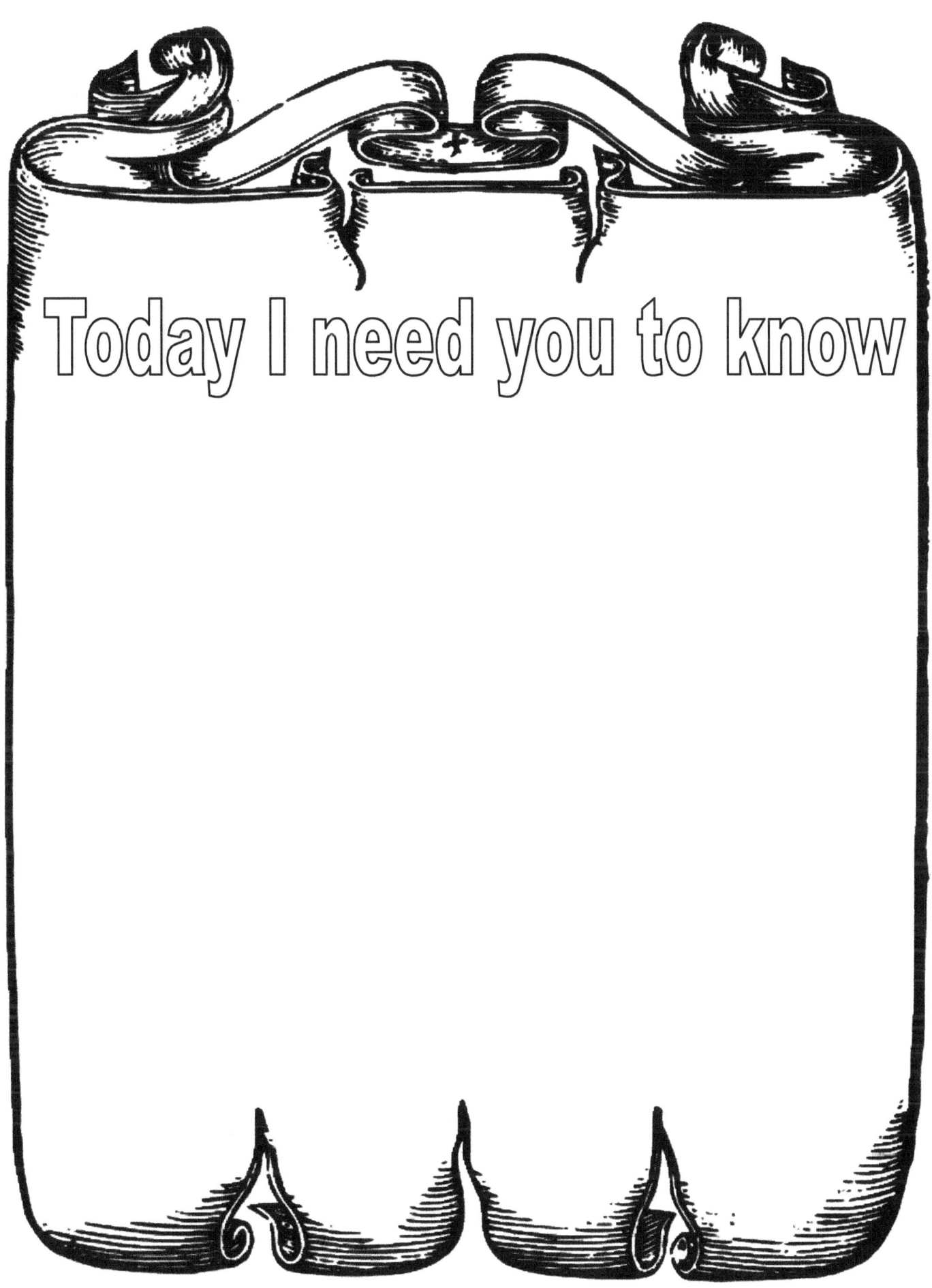

Today I need you to know

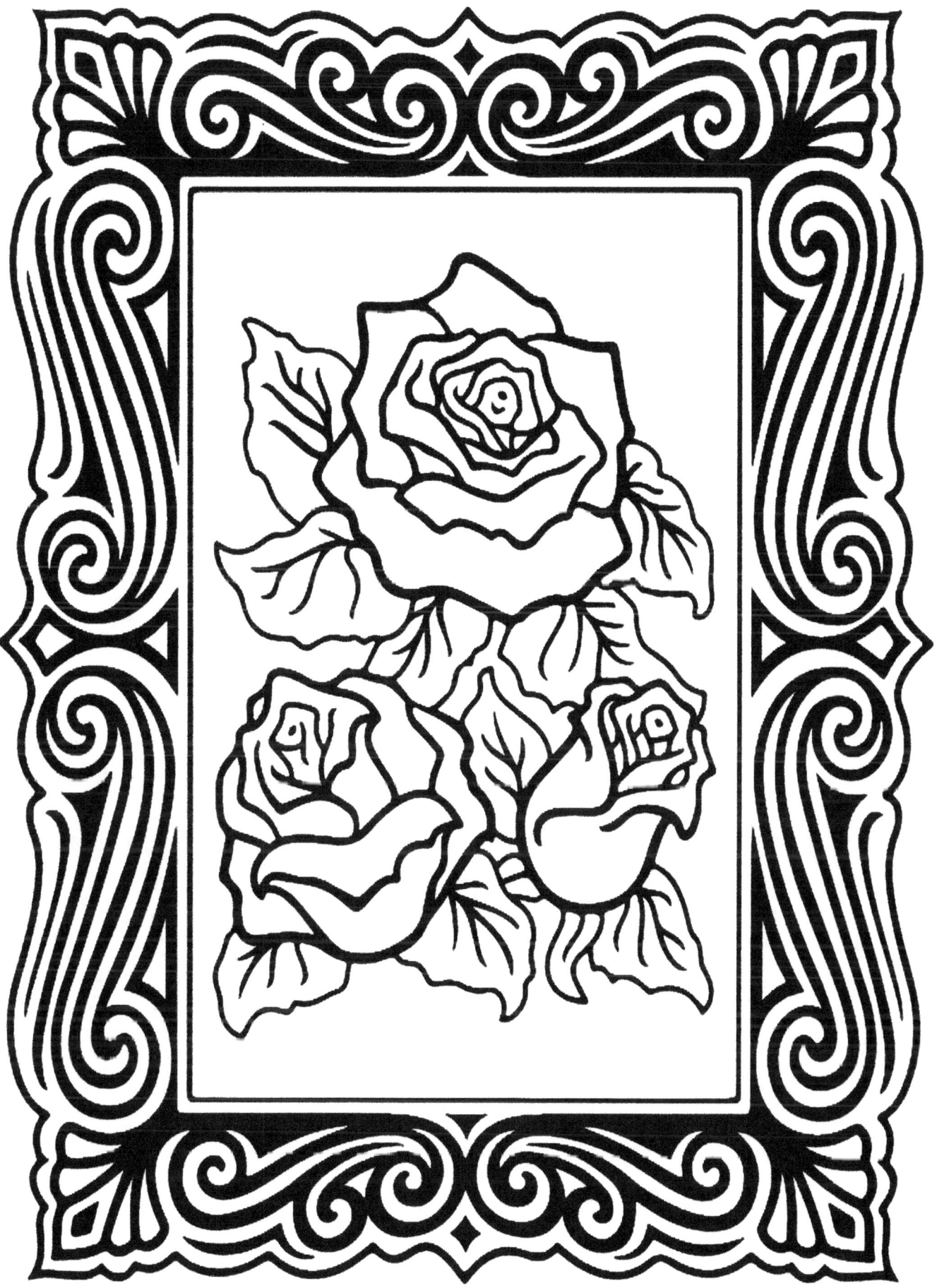

some times just being outside feels like too much

_____

_____

_____

_____

_____

_____

_____

_____

_____

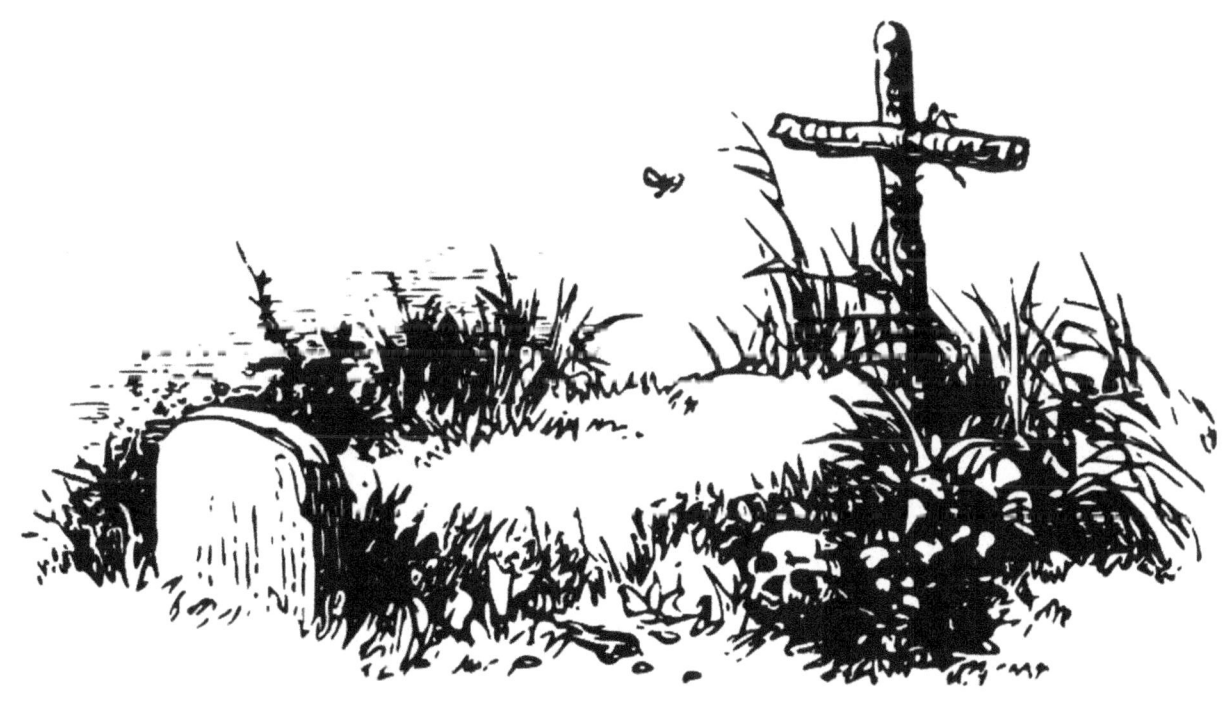

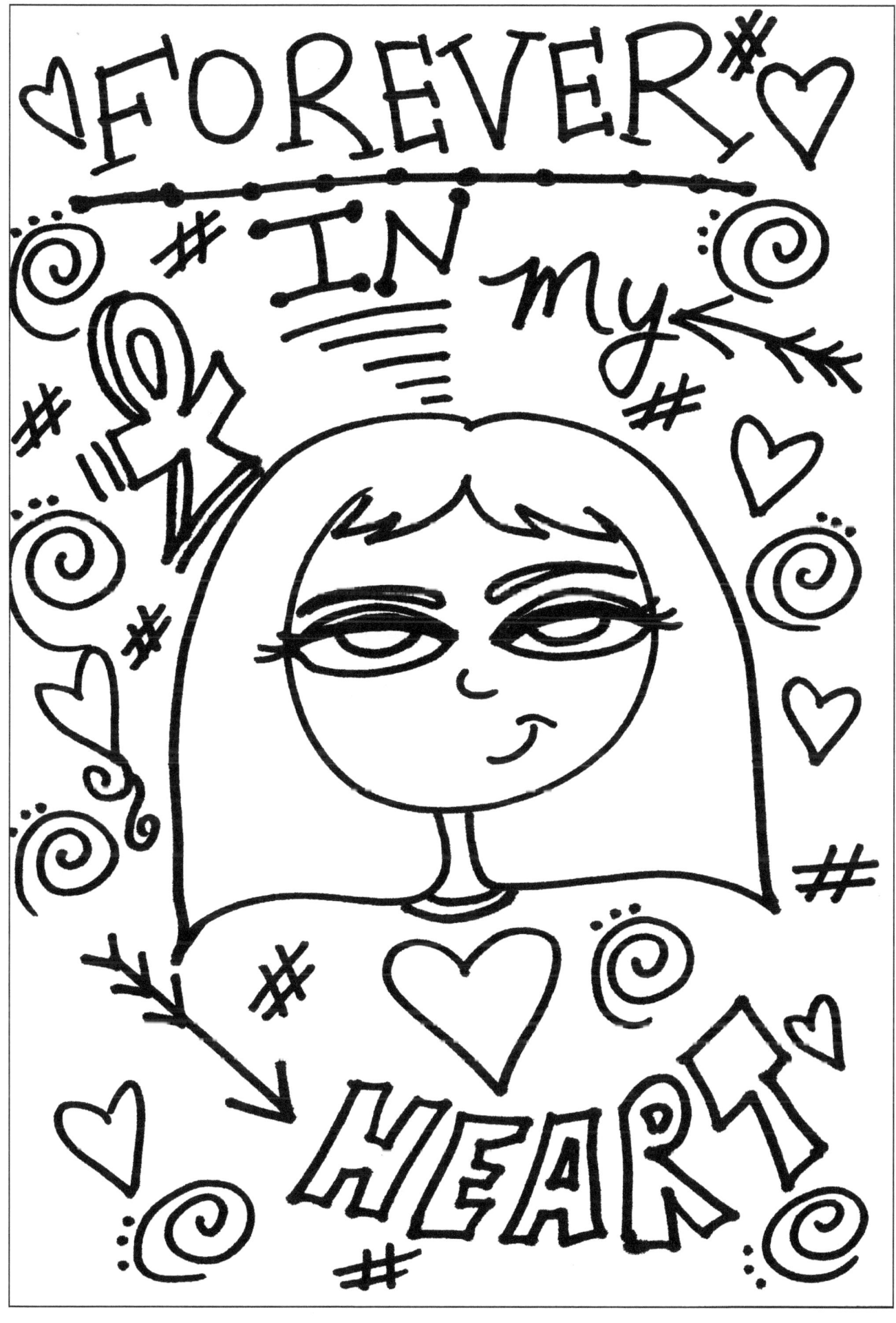

In this moment

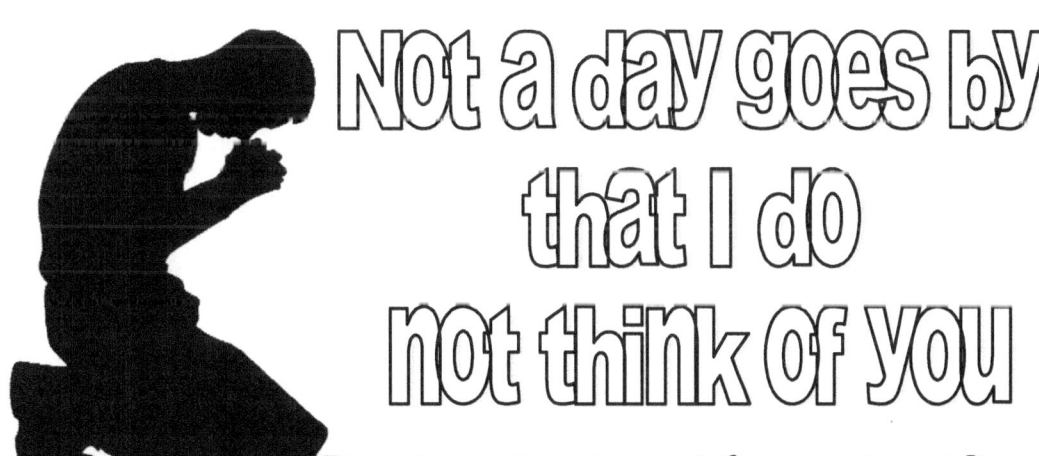

Not a day goes by that I do not think of you

Lighting a candle for you today
I miss you so much

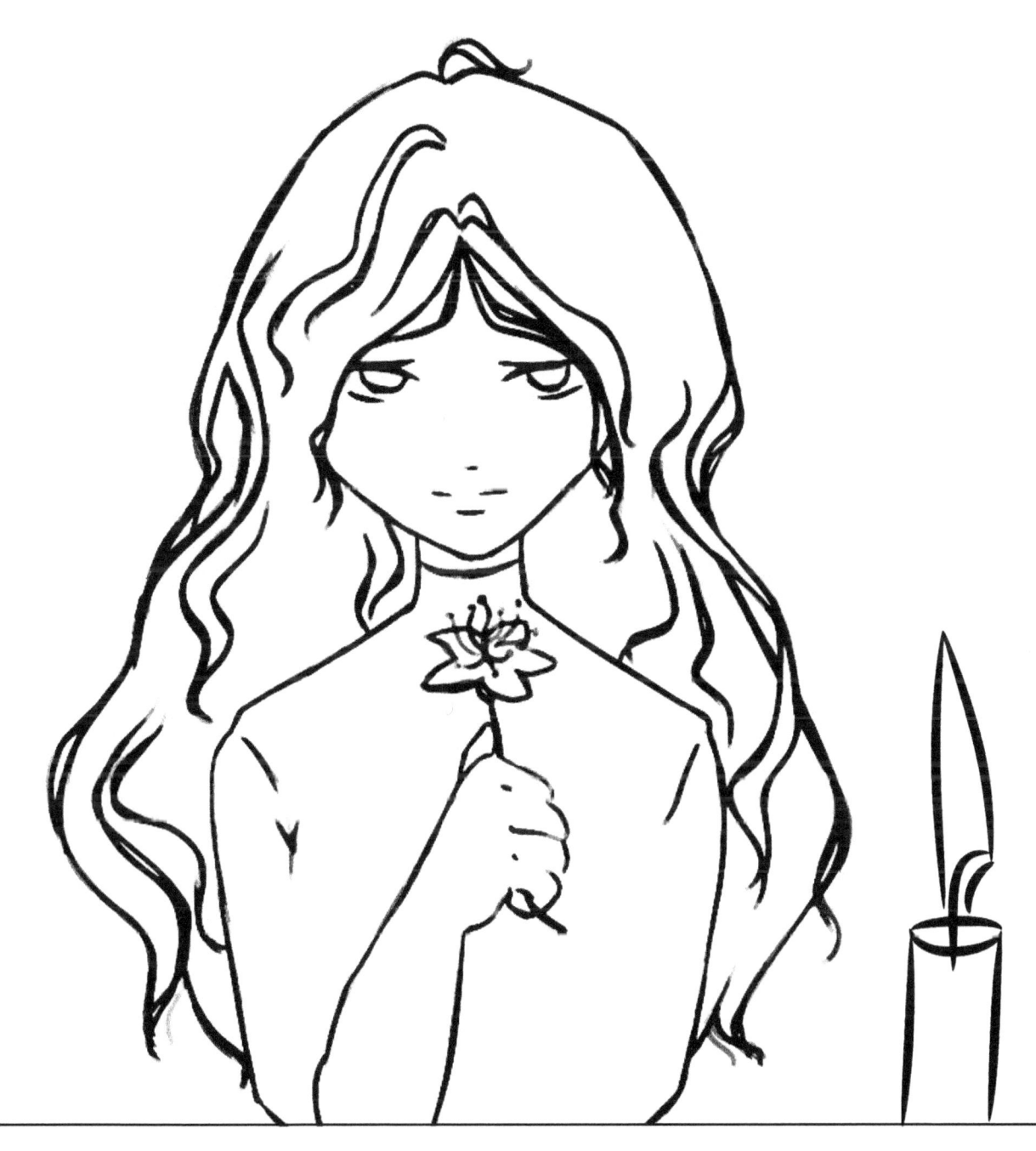

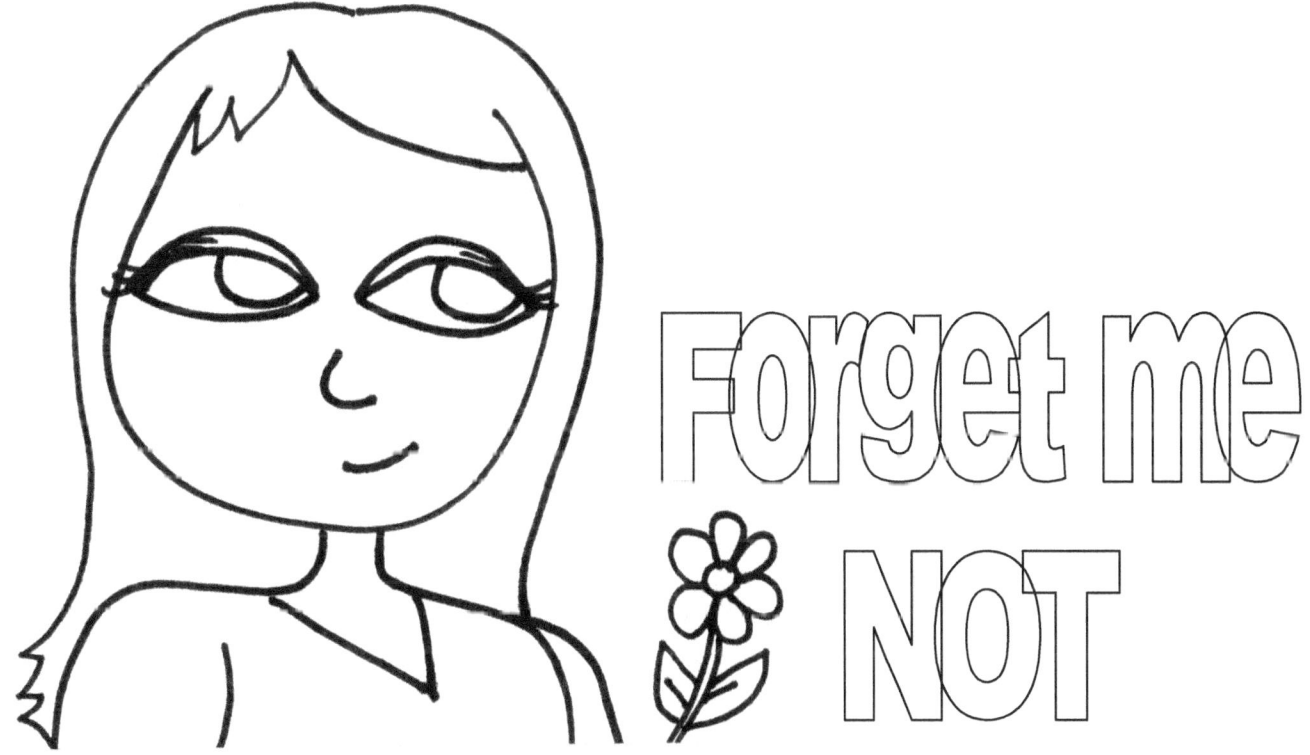

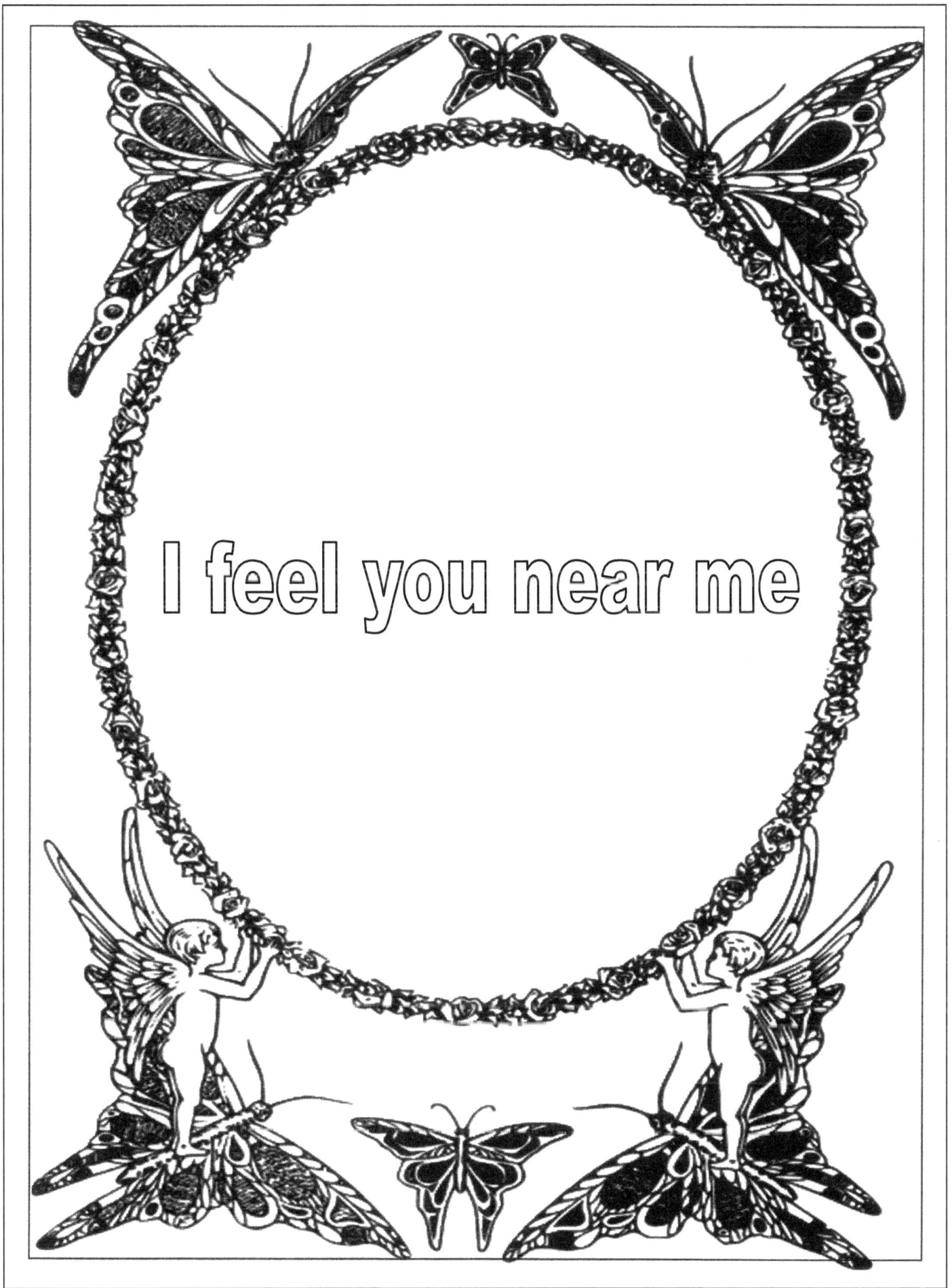

Some moments of grief feel unbearable. The longing to be with your loved one can take over so many moments we end up losing the appreciation for the present moment. Your loved one would not want you to continue to suffer. Your loved one would want you to live your life. You are still here after all. Channel your grief into positive action steps. Here are a few suggestions to help you in this stage of grief:

1) Light a candle everyday for 40 days. When you light the candle tell your say your loved one's name and share your loving energy with them.

2) Plant something! Plant a tree or a flower garden in honour of your loved one. Live in a smaller space? Purchase a smaller plant to have in your home.

3) Hold a Releasing Ceremony (see the final pages of this book)

4) Gather a few of their belongings (if you have them) and a picture or two. Place these on a small table; like an altar in their memory. Spend time remembering the good times.

5) Write a letter to your loved one. Fold it in half and place it under a tea-light candle. As you burn the candle know they are receiving your message.

6) Keep a journal (maybe on the blank pages of this book?) recording any dreams or messages you feel you have received from your loved one.

7) Go for a walk alone and talk to your loved one. Share what you are experiencing in that moment. Tell them how you feel. Walking changes the chemistry in our brains and helps us to feel better.

8) Create a memory box. Put belongs, pictures or anything you wish to keep of your loved one.

9) Write down things you want to remember about the day your loved one passed. Or the events which lead up to the passing. Put it in your memory box so you can revisit it years from now.

10) Join a bereavement group. Sometimes being with others who are in a similar place mentally does wonders. You are not alone!

11) Listen to your loved one's favourite music. Set up a playlist of their favourite songs. Listen, enjoy and sing!

12) Go for counselling. Seeing a Grief Counsellor can really help if you are struggling to move forward.

13) Honour yourself! Be patient and kind to you. This process is a journey which will shift and change. It's OK to feel what you are feeling!

Additional Ideas:

14) Have an upcoming family function? Save your loved one a chair; place flowers and a picture of them to honour their memory.

15) Start a blog or open a page on a social media site to record your favourite moments. Ask others to share their stories to leave as comments or by email so you can post it at some point.

16) Go for a walk by the water. On the walk pick up a stone for every bad feeling you are having. Find a place to sit near the water's edge and intend you are releasing these negative feelings as you toss the stones into the water. You may have to throw a lot of stones!

17) Near a campfire? Similar to the stone idea, pick up some fallen sticks to represent how you are feeling. Toss them into the fire and watch it burn away knowing it is helping you let go.

18) Buy some liquid bubbles. Think of the stage of grief you are in. Blow away the negative feelings. Watch the bubbles float away from you intending you are releasing with your breath.

19) Start a breathing practice. Use a simple technique saying to yourself, "Inhale light, exhale pain". Five minutes everyday. You don't have to sit and close your eyes. You can use this anywhere, anytime to help you to feel better. You don't even have to label the 'pain' as the subconscious mind knows what it is.

20) Go for a massage, a Reiki or another type of spa treatment. Just be nice to you!

21) Be present. Although this may sound clique it is the basis behind "This Stage of Grief" Give yourself permission to be here. The past is dust, the future is not promised but here, now, is guaranteed. Feel the sensations in your body, breathe and relax.

22) Learn a meditation technique. There are many ways to meditate: loving kindness, walking meditation, chakra meditation, breathing meditations... the list goes on and on. Find one that suits you or join a group to learn.

23) Make a list of positive affirmations to help you feel better. Put them on the fridge and read them often.

24) Write, "I love you" on post-it notes and place them randomly around the house. When you see them know you are loved and have loved. Be kind to yourself.

25) Visit with friends. Sometimes you just need to get out of your head. Create new memories.

26) Talk to your spirit guide. Even if you don't know their names (yes you have many). Ask them to help you get through this day. Remember to take one day at a time. Sometimes it will be one minute at a time; baby steps.

Releasing Ceremony

Supplies:

Lighter or matches

3 Candles (any colour or size)

3 tea-light candles (or more see below)

Picture of your loved one

Anything else you may wish to include

Timing:

There is not a wrong time to preform this ceremony. However many believe any time after a full moon before the moon comes new is best for releasing.

The Setting:

Place the photograph of your loved one before you.

If you are doing this with others you could sit around a table and place the picture of the loved one between you.

Light three candles (not the tea-lights just yet); arrange them where ever you wish.

Opening Ceremony

Read the Lord's Prayer or another prayer of your choosing that reverberates for you. You could ask Archangel Michael to wrap his protective wings around all of you.

The lighting of candles:

Light a tealight candle for your loved one saying, "I light this candle for_____" or something along these lines. Place the candle in front of your loved ones picture.

Next light a tealight candle for anyone in attendance saying the same for each. Place these candles near the first.

Step #1

Have a conversation with your loved one including anything you have not yet told them or wish to share.

Step #2

If you need to forgive, do so now. If you need to be forgiven ask for it now.

Step #3

Let your loved one know you are so grateful to have been part of their journey. Give thanks.

Step#4

Tell your loved one that although you'd love them to hang around and wish they would stay forever, it's time for them to cross over to the other side and prepare to do their life review.

Step #5

See them walking up a crystal staircase to heaven. Half way up see, sense, feel or imagine them turning around with a big smile to wave goodbye to you. You may say, "See you later", "see you in my dreams" or anything you feel guided to say to send them onto the next part of their journey.

Closing:

Repeat the opening prayer two times: Lord's Prayer or other

Let the tea-light candles burn themselves out. Know that you're loved one is still near and always will be. They are busy helping from the other side. You may call upon them at any time for their support.

Please note: There is no right or wrong way to preform a Releasing Ceremony; please modify or adjust this to your liking and make it your own!

About the Creator:

Tammy Lawrence-Cymbalisty is an Alternative Care provider working in the Kitchener/Waterloo Region. Since 2001 she has helped many people find peace, happiness, harmony and further purpose in their lives.

Tammy holds many degrees including: B.A. Sociology

(Trent University), Certified Yoga Teacher, Reiki

Master/Teacher, HypnoBirthing® Practitioner, Meditation Teacher, Workshop facilitator, Writer, Personal Growth Coach.

She lives with her husband, two felines and a school of fins in Cambridge, ON

Find out more by following Tammy on social media:

http://www.twitter.com/tllc

http://www.tinyurl.com/tlcservices

May you find peace

May you find happiness

May you be free from suffering

Namaste, Tammy

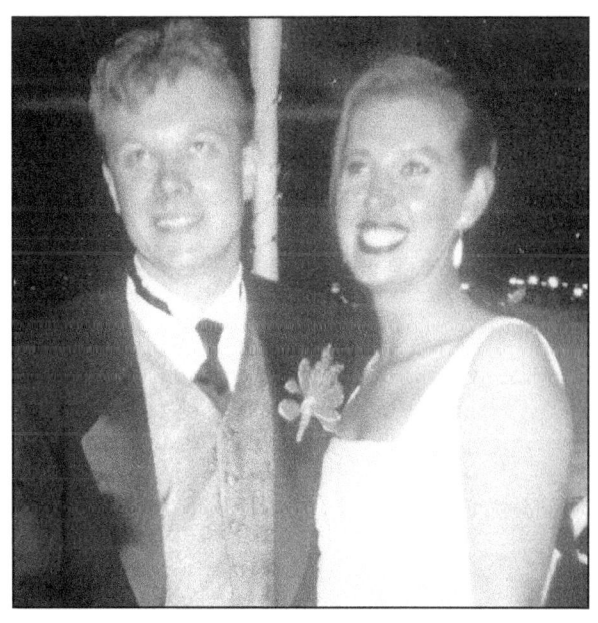

RIP David July 24/70 –March 13/15

And all others who passed before you.